CW00405950

flora

Edward Lucie-Smith

flora

GARDENS AND PLANTS IN ART AND LITERATURE

Page 2 illustration: Hunt Slonem, *Orchids* (1985)

EVERGREEN is an imprint of TASCHEN GmbH

The Ivy Press Limited
The Old Candlemakers, West Street
Lewes, East Sussex, BN7 2NZ
Art Director: Clare Barber
Editorial Director: Sophie Collins
Designer: Angela Neal
Project Editor: Rowan Davies
Editors: Claire Musters and April McCroskie
Picture Research: Liz Eddison

Cover design: Angelika Taschen, Cologne

Printed in China
ISBN 3–8228–5874–9

contents

introduction

"To me the meanest flower that blows can give
Thoughts that do often lie too deep for tears."

WILLIAM WORDSWORTH (1770–1850)

FLORA CELEBRATES the beauty of gardens and plants of all kinds. It explores the way that artists from diverse centuries and cultures have seen humankind's relationship with the vegetable kingdom—"the realm of Flora" as mythologists call it. Creating gardens has become the natural instinct of men and women who have long ceased to be nomadic. With the first fixed habitations came the beginnings of agriculture—the growing of plants for nourishment, or for use in other ways. The cultivation of soil, however, also evolved into an esthetic activity as men and women wanted to shape their surroundings so that they would provide both delight and solace.

John Frederick **LEWIS**
In the Bey's Garden
1865

Hunt **SLONEM**
Saint Rose of Lima (detail)
1989

Throughout history, a carefully cultivated garden has symbolized the control that the human race has learned to exercise over its surroundings. It shows that humans have the ability to control an unpredictable universe in some small way, by shaping the natural space around them with their own original ideas and designs. Gardens are usually fenced off, and so they can also be seen to reveal the basic human need for protection and shelter from the random violence of the world outside their encircling, safe boundary.

Lily **SALVO**
The Gate of Desire (detail)
1998

Art that has been inspired by gardens has faithfully reflected their tendency to challenge prevailing conditions. Dwellers in dry and desert locations, for example, have constantly sought the solace of water, so the presence and play of water—ponds, streams, rills, and fountains—have often become almost as important to their garden design as the plants that are cultivated there.

Alfredo
RAMOS MARTINEZ
Flower Sellers
1930s

Gardens have also tended to echo the prevailing intellectual climate of the civilizations that created them. In China, for example, garden design has reflected the three chief creeds that shape Chinese thought —Taoism, Confucianism, and Buddhism. All of these value contact with nature as something that helps to produce a state of spiritual calm. Visits to remote beauty spots were not always a practical possibility, so Chinese gardens tried to reproduce the physical features of these admired landscapes, and the emotions they evoked.

The civilization of Europe, centreing on man's dominance of his surroundings rather than on the supremacy of nature, tended to see garden design as an extension of the art of architecture. This began to change with the rise of the art of landscape painting during the seventeenth century, but attitudes to gardens and to the cultivation of both ornamental and useful plant species were also affected by a

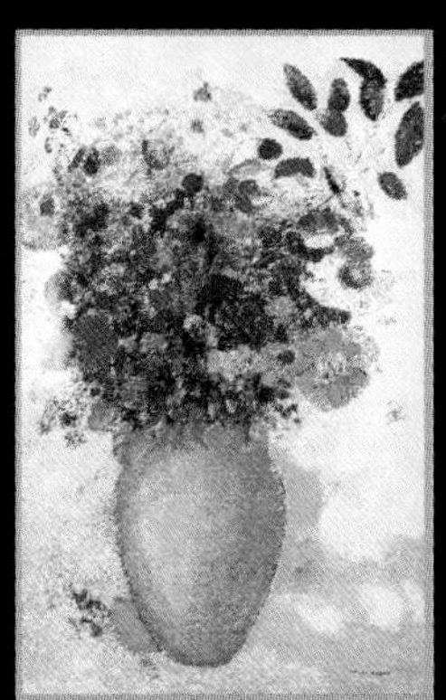

Odilon
REDON
Flowers in a Turquoise Vase
1905

new scientific spirit, linked to the desire for geographical exploration. European gardens became repositories for the plants that explorers brought back. By 1656, for instance, the catalog of the Tradescant family's private botanical garden in London listed 1,600 different species. Among them were the New York aster, goldenrod, and Virginia creeper—plants from the New World which were previously unknown in Europe. Later, in the eighteenth century, under the influence of Jean-Jacques Rousseau (1712–78), philosophy became obsessed with a new enthusiasm for "nature" and "the natural" as all-embracing concepts.

Joseph-Marie **VIEN**
Greek Youth Crowning His Beloved with Flowers (detail)
1773

The realm of flora celebrated here in art involves both long historical perspectives and wild flights of fancy. Artists have often made minute examinations of the infinitely varied treasures that nature has to offer. Indeed, in art, the commonplace and the exotic can be equally precious. And contemporary gardeners are as keenly aware of this as their predecessors.

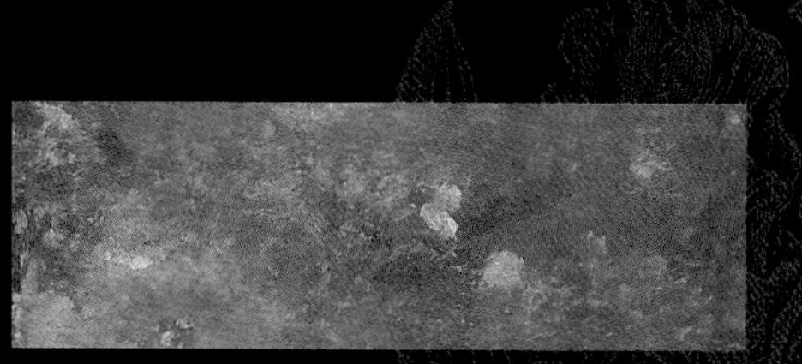

CHAPTER ONE

the mirror of paradise

"A Garden was the Habitation of our first Parents before the Fall. It is naturally apt to fill the Mind with Calmness and Tranquillity."

JOSEPH ADDISON (1672–1719)

Alfred **ROLL**
The Joys of Life: Flowers, Women, Music (Mural)
c. 1877

GARDENS HAVE ALWAYS been seen as reflections of paradise—the perfect location for an ultimately desirable state of being. Christian doctrine holds that human beings were once in possession of just such a state, but were deprived of it through their own disobedience and foolishness. Muslims believe that everything the heroes of the faith (those who sacrifice their lives for Islam) can desire after death will be provided for them in the most perfect of gardens.

Paradise, miniature from a Bruges School manuscript c. 1500

The locations where perfect happiness is to be found differ considerably between cultures and religions. In the imaginations of early Christian artists, Eden seems to have resembled one of the hunting parks created in pre-Christian times by the despotic rulers of the Ancient Near East—the Assyrians and their successors the Achamaenid rulers of Persia. They inherited this vision

from the Jewish creators of the Old Testament, some of whom must have seen such parks in reality. As we know from the Assyrian palace reliefs found at Nineveh and elsewhere, these hunting parks were places where scenes of savage cruelty took place, as game captured or bred was mercilessly slaughtered by the king and his attendants. Biblical Eden reverses the situation, making the park a place where all species of birds and animals can live in perfect harmony, both with one another and with humans, their most dangerous predators.

Ivan **RABUZIN**
Peaceful Road in the Woods
1921

Spring, illustration to the "Tacuinium Sanitatis in medicina"
North Italian
Late 14th century

The Muslim attitude to paradise was a response to the desert conditions that most of the great Muslim rulers were familiar with. In the fourteenth century, Tamerlane founded no less than eleven royal gardens near his capital of Samarkand. The Emperor Babur (1483–1530), founder of the Mogul Empire, recorded in his memoirs his appreciation of the lushness he found when he descended into India from his headquarters in Afghanistan. After he won his first great Indian victory at Panipat in 1525, one of his first actions was to create a garden, the Ram Bagh, at Agra. It was in fact his custom to create gardens wherever he went and to use them as a setting for convivial parties, where poetry and wine were enjoyed in equal measure.

Arthur **DIXON**
The King's Garden or the Harvest of Labour
c. 1900

Judy **BYFORD**
Dream Garden
(detail)
1994

Due to the uncertainty of political conditions, medieval gardens were essentially enclosed, protected spaces, very limited in extent, where the aristocratic inhabitants of a heavily fortified castle could take the air while staying within a safe area. These spaces were usually dedicated to

women, and the "hortus conclusus," or peacefully enclosed garden, became particularly associated with the Virgin. Often such gardens were raised well above ground level, on the summit of some turret, and thus had affinities with the so-called "hanging gardens" of ancient Babylon, which were built on high terraces. Generally divided symmetrically into four parts, with a well or some other feature at the center, medieval gardens did contain flowers, but the number of species was limited and the flowering season very short. Another version of the medieval garden—the enclosed courtyard, with buildings on all sides—was inherited from the ancient world. It became especially typical in monasteries, where it took the form of a cloister or covered walk enclosing a green space. This has been passed down to the present day as a typical formula for urban gardens.

Stefano da **VERONA** *The Madonna of the Rose Garden* (detail) 1425

"*All the trees they are so high,*
The leaves they are so green."

ANONYMOUS

The Emperor Babur Receiving Envoys in a Garden, Mogul
c. 1590

The Emperor Babur (ruled 1526–30) loved gardens, and he is shown here receiving envoys outside the walls of Agra, in the year 1528. The exquisite setting, with its flowering trees, has a strong political message—it illustrates his power to make nature blossom at his command.

François **BOUCHER**
The Chinese Garden
c. 1725–50

Such fanciful European interpretations of Chinese styles were closely associated with the Rococo. They formed the bridge between Rococo artificiality and the new interest in nature. Boucher's (1703–70) painting portrays a charming pastoral fairyland that never existed in reality.

Ivan **RABUZIN**
Peaceful Road in the Woods
date unknown

Fascination with the work of Henri Rousseau (1844–1910) led to a fascination with the work of untutored artists in general. There was a flourishing school of them in Yugoslavia between World War I and II. This visionary landscape by Rabuzin (b. 1921) is a typical example of this.

Paradise, miniature from a Bruges School manuscript
c. 1500

This illustration comes from a book on the Seven Wonders of the World and shows Adam and Eve in the Garden of Eden before the Fall. God the Father presides above them.

“Babylon… somewhat answering or hinting the old opinion concerning Paradise itself, with many conceptions elevated above the plane of earth.”

SIR THOMAS BROWNE (1605–82)

Woodcut after
Ferdinand von **KNAB**
The Hanging Gardens of Babylon
1886

The religious revival of the early nineteenth century prompted attempts by artists to visualize the settings described in the Bible. This is a would-be antiquarian reconstruction of the palace of the Chaldean King of Babylon Nebuchadnezzar II (c. 630–c. 561BC). Jeremiah and Ezekiel both regarded him as God's chosen instrument. In the Book of Daniel he is described as going mad and eating grass.

OBERRHEINISCHER MEISTER
Garden of Paradise
Early 15th century

This delightful panel in the International Gothic style shows the Virgin seated in a garden reading a book while the infant Jesus plays a psaltery (the ancestor of the harpsichord). This instrument is held for him by a female saint. Angels and human attendants are also present, wearing the fashionable dress of the day.

“*The Christ-child stood at Mary's knee,*
His hair was like a crown,
And all the flowers looked up at Him,
And all the stars looked down.”

G. K. CHESTERTON (1874–1936)

Stefano da **VERONA**
The Madonna of the Rose Garden
1425

In late medieval art the Madonna is often represented in a rose garden. Here, the fact that she sits directly on the ground is emblematic of her humility, while the roses themselves symbolize sweetness and purity, thereby also emphasizing these qualities in her.

The Sense of Taste
Tapestry from "The Lady with the Unicorn" series
15th century

From a famous series of tapestries now in the Musée Cluny in Paris. Medieval legend stated that the unicorn could be caught only by a virgin; it would lay its head in her lap and allow itself to be led to the king's palace. The tapestry is in the *mille-fleurs* style ("thousand flowers"), which takes its name from the tradition of creating the background of a work with plants and flowers.

> *Stay quiet; refuse nothing; flowers only grow because they tranquilly allow the sun's rays to reach them. You must do the same.*
>
> **JULIA KRUDENER** (1764–1824)

Spring, illustration to the "Tacuinium Sanitatis in medicina," North Italian
Late 14th century

The "Tacuinium Sanitatis" is an early medical treatise, but this lyrical image has nothing to do with medicine. Rather, its purpose is to lift the spirits after the end of a long European winter.

"

Paradise were meeter far
To entertain so bright a star:
But why errs my folly so?
Paradise is where you are:
Heav'n above, and heav'n below.

"

THOMAS CAMPION (1567–1620)

Loyset **LIEDET** and
Renaud de **MONTAUBAN**
The Garden of Love
Mid-15th century

This garden scene exemplifies the tradition of the Courts of Love that were founded by Eleanor of Aquitaine (c. 1122–1204) in the twelfth century. The garden that surrounds the lovers is symbolic of their exclusive love for one another.

Salvo **RUSSO**
Pomegranates
1997

The wicker basket has been placed on a ledge that overlooks a prospect of sea and mountains. It is filled with fruit that is traditionally symbolic of the goddess of love. A pomegranate, floating in the sky, has taken the place of the rising moon, signifying that this is a night for love.

> *Here at the fountain's sliding foot,*
> *Or at some fruit-tree's mossy root...*
> *My soul into the boughs does glide:*
> *There like a bird it sits, and sings...*

ANDREW MARVELL (1621–78)

Judy **BYFORD**
Dream Garden
1994

A contemporary image that owes much to nineteenth-century folk art models, especially samplers, but which also includes a touch of the light-hearted eroticism that is more typical of our own day.

Wall-painting of a dove in a garden with a fountain, Pompeii

1st century AD

Prosperous Roman houses were often adorned with murals representing gardens. They were especially popular in dining-rooms, and were meant to give those feasting the illusion that they were in fact enjoying their meal in the idyllic outdoors.

Women in a Garden Pavilion
Indian, Basholi School
c. 1650–75

This illustration to an Indian romance is typical of the paintings made in the foothills of the Himalayas, with their intense response to nature. The gesturing woman asks her companion: "Where would we find a spot other than this for our embraces?"

Hank **PITCHER**
Adam and Eve
1987

Adam and Eve are screened by bamboo stems and hibiscus plants in full bloom. They are by implication primitive tribespeople, ignorant of the troubles of modern urban society.

Rug with Adam and Eve, Jewish
19th century

Made in Turkey, this rug illustrates the Book of Genesis. The central scene is the Fall; the borders of the rug contain the story of Cain and Abel. The rug breaks both Jewish and Islamic prohibitions against figurative representation.

> "*And even with Paradise devise the Snake.*"
>
> **EDWARD FITZGERALD** (1809–83)

Miniature illustrating the story of Adam and Eve, from a French translation of Boccaccio's "On the Fates of Famous Men" (1355–74) and "Concerning Famous Women" (1360–74)
1465

There are four episodes contained in this work, starting at the top left with the Creation of Eve, followed by the Fall, the Expulsion from Paradise, and finally a scene showing Adam digging and Eve spinning.

"

Consider how the lilies grow... not even Solomon in all his splendour was dressed like one of these.

"

LUKE 12:27

Arthur **DIXON**
The King's Garden or the Harvest of Labour (detail)
c. 1900

This late Pre-Raphaelite work represents a medieval dreamworld in which everyone is virtuous. This is symbolized by the field of white lilies, interspersed with a few roses, which grows before the castle gate.

Antoine **WATTEAU**
The Feast of Love
1717

A typical Watteau (1684–1721) *fête champêtre,* where elegantly dressed couples flirt beside a statue of Venus in a park. Venus is endeavoring to restrain her son Cupid, by taking his arrows away from him. The implication is that the mortals who surround her are in enough trouble already.

> "*The Book of Life begins… in a garden… It ends with Revelations.*"
>
> **OSCAR WILDE** (1854–1900)

Lucas **CRANACH**
Adam and Eve in the Garden of Eden (detail)
Early 16th century

Cranach (1472–1553) follows medieval examples (*see page 35*) by illustrating several episodes from the story of the Fall on the same canvas. The main episode is not the actual temptation scene, but God admonishing the couple.

CHAPTER TWO

sowing and reaping

"He sends the snow in winter
The warmth to swell the grain
The breezes and the sunshine,
And soft refreshing rain."

JANE MONTGOMERY CAMPBELL (1817–78)

Claude **MONET**
The Grainstacks
1891

THE SEASONAL LABORS of sowing and reaping became an integral part of the established repertoire of art at a very early date. Ancient Egypt, with its settled agricultural society, had a deep conviction that the afterlife would simply be a mirror image of the life lived here on earth. The highly detailed tomb painting and reliefs of this civilization provide illustrations of the way in which the most essential crops were cultivated in the Valley of the Nile, with the aid of the annual inundation.

Alexander
MANN
The Gleaners
1881

In more northern climates—for example, continental Europe—the pattern was different from Egypt. Four seasons were recognized (spring, summer, fall, and winter) and there were agricultural and pastoral activities appropriate not only to each season but to each month. These activities became favorite themes for artists to

Pierre-Auguste
RENOIR
The Reaper
(detail)
1873

illustrate in the new type of devotional book that was introduced in the middle of the thirteenth century. Linked to the ever more fervent cult of the Virgin Mary, this book contained prayers that were to be said in her honor at each of the appropriate canonical hours. It soon became customary to add a calendar of saints' days to these texts, accompanied by minutely detailed miniatures illustrating the labors of the months. The most celebrated book of this type is *Les Très Riches Heures*, which was produced at the beginning of the fifteenth century for Jean Duc de Berry by the Flemish artist Pol de Limbourg and his brothers. This particular book depicts the Duke's principal residences and portrays the rhythm of life both within and without their walls.

John William
WATERHOUSE
The Orange Gatherers
(detail)
date unknown

The Limbourgs' chief successor in handling this theme was another Fleming, Pieter Bruegel the Elder (c. 1525–69). Bruegel's *Labors of the Months* are not illustrations for a prayer book but are independent paintings on panels. They are more sophisticated than the Limbourgs' work and reveal Bruegel's knowledge of Italian Renaissance art, which he had seen at first hand during a voyage to Italy. What he has in common with the Limbourgs, however, is not just his keen observation of the seasonal round, but his somewhat distanced view of peasant life.

Calendar Miniature for the Month of October, Bedford Hours
c. 1423

August **MACKE**
Tree in a Cornfield
(detail)
1907

His patrons, like the Limbourgs, were great aristocrats, and for them the life of the soil, though familiar in one sense since it flourished in their pre-industrial society, was somewhat removed from their own lives and was seen as "exotic." The tendency to idealize peasant life was inherited by many later European artists, among them Gainsborough, Constable, and Stubbs. Perhaps the first artist to actually experience the life of a peasant before painting it was Jean-François Millet (1814–75). However, even his work is essentially an idealization, although it does also stress the hardships of peasant life.

The European consciousness of an inexorable seasonal rhythm within nature was expressed in the story of the Green Man, most familiar to us now through the great Middle English poem *Sir Gawayne and the Greene Knight*, which is thought to have been written c. 1375. In this poem the mysterious Green Knight arrives at King Arthur's court and offers to accept any type of blow from any man if he can return the stroke to him a year later. Sir Gawayne accepts the challenge and decapitates the knight, but is horrified to see the mysterious challenger pick up his head and depart. This strange knight is actually a personification of corn, which is cut down every year, then grows again.

Camille
PISSARRO
Spring
(detail)
1872

August **MACKE**
Tree in a Cornfield
1907

This painting, by the short-lived August Macke (1887–1914) who was killed in the early months of World War I, shows the impact made on German art by French Impressionism. Macke, who was a member of the Blaue Reiter group formed in Munich in 1911, is here slowly feeling his way toward a new and more subjective style, which was later to become known as Expressionism.

John William **WATERHOUSE**
The Orange Gatherers
date unknown

Waterhouse (1849–1917) generally preferred to paint classical scenes or illustrations to literature, like his ever-popular *Lady of Shallott*, now in the Tate Gallery, London. In this Italian genre scene he follows in the footsteps of his more eminent contemporary Lord Leighton (1830–96), another specialist in classicism who relaxed by making elegant sketches of Italian landscapes.

> "*In paradise is the plant that*
> *springs in the open*
> *When the dripping dew drops*
> *from its leaves*"

FROM SIR GAWAYNE AND THE GREENE KNIGHT

A Northern Swiss Tapestry frieze illustrating a grass-covered woodman leaving his wife to hunt a stag with his hounds
1468–76

In this medieval tapestry the green leaves in the huntsman's hair characterize him as the Green Man—or Green Knight—who is the descendant of the old Celtic God of Nature; cut down every fall to be reborn every spring. The woman's leafy costume is also emblematic of nature.

> *Ah Sun-flower!... Who countest the steps of the Sun*
>
> **WILLIAM BLAKE** (1757–1827)

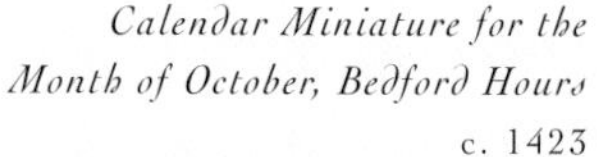

Calendar Miniature for the Month of October, Bedford Hours
c. 1423

This figure of a man sowing comes from a Book of Hours made for John, Duke of Bedford (1389–1435) who was chief English commander in France after the death of his brother Henry V. The man's dress suggests that he has a purely allegorical function rather than belonging to the peasant class.

Robert **BISSEL**
The Stand
1997

Bissel's (b. 1952) rabbit, contemplating a row of gigantic sunflowers, has some of the dream-like magic of the illustrations of Sir John Tenniel (1820–1914) for Lewis Carroll's (1832–98) *Alice in Wonderland* (1865) and *Alice Through the Looking Glass* (1872). Sunflowers are, however, cultivated—in Egypt and India as well as in Europe—chiefly for their seeds, which yield an oil in many ways equivalent to olive oil. The leaves are used as fodder and the sunflower oil cake left, after pressing the oil, is fed to poultry.

Pieter **BRUEGEL THE YOUNGER**
Summer
c. 1622–35

The composition for this painting derives from one of the famous series depicting the seasons, which were painted by the artist's father, Pieter Bruegel the Elder (c.1525–69). Bruegel the Elder, in turn, relied on similar scenes that appear in fifteenth-century *Books of Hours*. Here, the heat of summer is symbolized by the hay harvest, with one of the harvesters drinking thirstily in the right foreground. The patrons of the Bruegels, father and sons, were courtly aristocrats, who regarded peasants such as those shown here as strange outlandish creatures, little better than beasts.

Nancy **SMITH**
Man Digging Vegetables
c. 1945

This London Transport poster is eloquent concerning the ambiguous relationship between country and town. Essentially the townee is being urged to take a trip to the outskirts, in order to enjoy the unaccustomed sight of people tilling the soil. The style of the poster, with its flat areas of color, owes a good deal to the much earlier poster work of William Nicholson (1872–1949) and James Pryde (1869–1941), who worked together in the Edwardian period, calling themselves the Beggarstaff Brothers.

George **STUBBS**
The Harvest Wagon
1770s

Stubbs' (1724–1806) representations of harvesting scenes and other rural activities were an extension of his work as a sporting and animal painter. Notable here is the precise geometry of the composition, with the harvest wagon itself placed parallel to the picture plane so that, with its attendant figures, it forms the basis for the modern equivalent of a neo-classical frieze. The neatness of the figures themselves stresses the prosperity of English agriculture at this time.

Alexander **MANN**
The Gleaners (detail)
1881

The little-known Scottish artist Alexander Mann (1853–1908) went to Paris to study in 1877. While there, he seems to have come into contact with the work of the French Impressionists, as this painting demonstrates. Scottish artists of this period were often more aware of new developments on the Continent than their English contemporaries. Grain is here being harvested in a still-traditional fashion—cut by hand, bound into sheaves, and finally loaded onto a horse-drawn wagon.

Camille **PISSARRO**
Spring
1872

This ambitious composition from Pissarro's (1830–1903) most successful Impressionist period shows peasants sowing. As the contemporary critic Théodore Duret recognized, Pissarro was the Impressionist most closely akin to the great Realist painter a generation older than himself, Jean-François Millet (1814–75). Of all the leading Impressionists, Pissarro was the most involved in politics; he was a lifelong Socialist, with a keen sympathy for the lives lived by the peasants who were so often his subjects.

"*The thirsty earth soaks up the rain,*
And drinks, and gapes for drink again.
The plants suck in the earth, and are
With constant drinking fresh and fair."

ABRAHAM COWLEY (1618–67)

Harvest Jug, earthenware with sgraffito decoration
c. 1813

Made using a technique that had changed little, if at all, since the Middle Ages, this harvest jug seems to celebrate the vintage rather than the corn-harvest, since it is decorated with vines.

Farmers at Work, Northern Sung Dynasty
AD 960–1279

This fresco comes from the Mogoa Caves, near Tun-Huang, which was at the far-western limit of Chinese settlement along the Silk Road that led eventually to Europe.

"
...they rejoice before yo
rejoice at the har
"

ISAIAH 9:2

BOUCICAUT MASTER
[and workshop]
Pepper Harvest in Coilum, Southern India
c. 1410

Spices were of great interest to people in the fourteenth century, not merely because of their exotic origins and corresponding high price, but because of the difficulty of preserving meat through the long winter months. The painter has represented a scene here he can never have witnessed himself, being European.

Charles **ANGRAND**
The Harvest
1887

Angrand (1854–1926) began as a follower of the Impressionists and then became a Pointillist under the influence of Georges Seurat (1859–91). Seurat's main objective in his painting was to give the Impressionist technique of dividing colors and building up forms out of little touches of pure hues a systematic, quasi-scientific basis. Angrand here takes the same subject matter as Monet's (1840–1926) *The Grainstacks* (although his painting is in fact earlier than Monet's celebrated series), and produces a rather stiff composition that reduces nature to an arrangement of geometrical forms.

Simon **BENING**
Vintage Scene
c. 1513–15

This picture, which comes from the Grimani Breviary, now housed in the library of San Marco in Venice, is essentially an update of similar scenes found in the *Très Riches Heures du Duc de Berry,* painted by the Limbourg brothers a century earlier. Like many of the pictures in the *Très Riches Heures,* it contrasts the lives of the laboring poor with the grand habitations occupied by their masters.

Pierre-Auguste **RENOIR**
The Reaper
1873

Renoir (1841–1919) ventured relatively seldom into agricultural scenes of this sort. This painting, produced early in the development of Impressionism, is notable for the informality of its composition, and its fresh, breezy atmosphere. There are few harvesters in the picture and their work does not seem to be especially energetic or intensive. Renoir was essentially not interested in the idea of labor. The figures he has included are incidental grace notes in his portrayal of a wide landscape.

Renoir. 73.

Edward **STOTT**
A French Kitchen Garden
1883

An English Realist touched by some knowledge of French Symbolism, Stott (1859–1918) exaggerates the scale of the cabbages growing in this kitchen garden, and diminishes the scale of the figure, in order to produce a more dramatic and ominous effect. Another influence on the way the composition has been constructed may have been photography, since the camera lens tends to exaggerate the scale of objects in the foreground.

Richard **LOPEZ**
Radicchio
1996

This artist lives and works in Southern California, and the intense light seen in the work is very reminiscent of that area. Extreme, quasi-abstract close-up views of flowers and plants were a gift to painting from photography. One of the first painters to create compositions of this sort was Georgia O'Keeffe (1887–1986), who seems to have borrowed the idea from the photographer Paul Strand (1890–1976), with whom she had a brief love affair. Radicchio, now fashionable as a salad vegetable, is a variety of chicory, and has striking, dark red-colored leaves.

Alsace Tapestry, Sowing
15th century

Here, one peasant is using a horse-drawn harrow to prepare the ground, while another sows. The tapestry belongs to a series showing the traditional *Labors of the Months*, in this case November rather than October, as in the similar scene from the *Bedford Hours* (*see page 50*).

Arthur **MELVILLE**
Cabbage Garden
1877

With its deep foreground, this realist work shows the influence of photography. The rural tranquility it portrays contrasts with the fact that Britain was, at the time this painting was done, the world's leading industrial power.

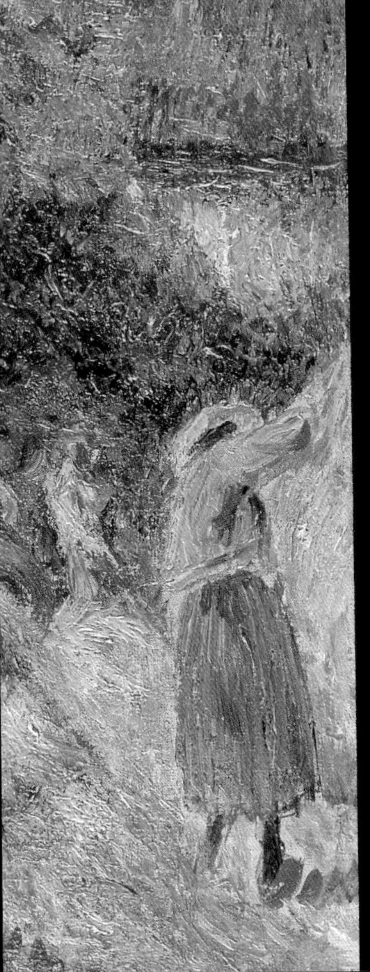

And those who husbanded the Golden Grain,
And those who flung it to the Winds like Rain,
Alike to no such aureate Earth are turn'd
As, buried once, men want dug up again.

EDWARD FITZGERALD (1809–83)

Camille **PISSARRO**
The Harvest (detail)
1882

In the early 1880s Pissarro (1830–1903) had a stylistic crisis. This painting, despite its official title, shows not the corn-harvest but the building of a haystack. When compared with the earlier painting by Pissarro in this section (*see pages 56–7*), there is a much greater emphasis on concerted human activity here. The huge haystack forces the spectator to concentrate on the activity of the figures in the foreground.

Sennedjem and His Wife in the Fields, Ancient Egypt
19th Dynasty, 1297–1185BC

This painting comes from the tomb of a high official of the Ramesside period. In one sense what it shows is unlikely; the owner of the tomb and his wife, in their best clothes, plowing and sowing. The Ancient Egyptians felt that the afterlife would be more or less exactly like the lives they had already lived, which is the reason that so many everyday activities are depicted in tomb-paintings. On the other hand, they also felt that agriculture was a sacred activity—the fundamental basis of society—which would account for the tomb-owners having themselves portrayed in this way.

Paul **CÉZANNE**
Summer
1859–62

This is one of a set of murals depicting the *Four Seasons* painted by Cézanne (1839–1906) for the entrance hall of the Jas de Bouffan, his family home. At the time he completed this work he was not much more than an amateur painter. His strong-minded father had forced him to study law at the University of Aix-en-Provence, though he did go to Paris for five months in 1861, returning home deeply discouraged by his own lack of technical facility. Here, it is not the clumsy figure but the incidentals—the basket of fruit, the cut melon, the sheaves of corn— that give promise of the marvels to come.

> *As is the Gardener,*
> *so is the Garden.*

THOMAS FULLER (1732)

Man Teaching a Rustic in a Herb Garden, Bruges
1473–83

This is from a manuscript illuminated in Flanders for the English king Edward IV (who reigned 1461–70 and 1471–83). Edward's sister Margaret was married to Charles the Bold, Duke of Burgundy, and the alliance gave Edward access to the workshops of Flemish illuminators. The picture comes from an early work on agricultural theory.

Vincent **VAN GOGH**
Red Vineyards at Arles
1888

Van Gogh (1853–90) left Paris for Arles in February 1888, and this picture dates from the latter part of his stay there. The grape-pickers are working in the vineyards under a setting sun that turns the whole scene wine-red, with the hay harvest going on beyond. These details show that the work was completed before Gauguin's (1848–1903) arrival in October, because the vintage would have been over by then. This work reveals the way in which Van Gogh was able to suffuse landscape with personal feeling and makes a striking contrast to Simon Bening's impersonal depiction of the same scene, reproduced on page 64.

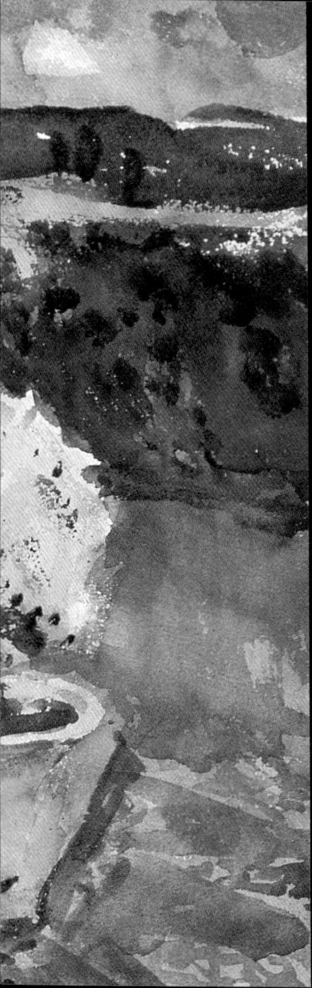

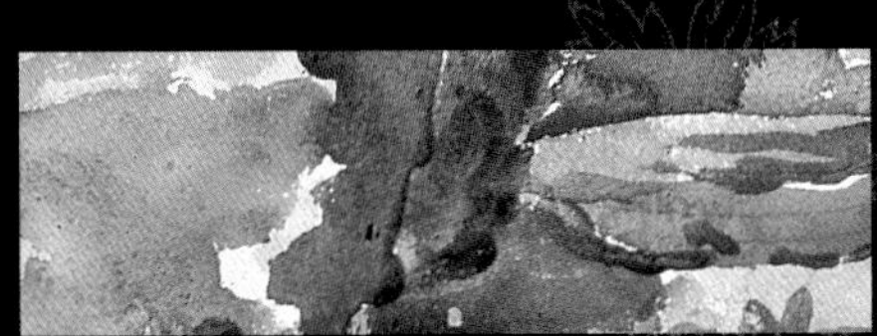

CHAPTER THREE

art versus nature

"There is continual spring, and harvest there
... for both the boughs do laughing blossoms bear

EDMUND SPENSER (c. 1552–99)

John Singer **SARGENT**
Fountains in the Generalife
c. 1910–20

THE CREATION OF GARDENS inevitably meant that gardeners were not only working with nature but, in some respects, actually working in opposition to it. The so-called "knot gardens," which adorned the terraces of great Elizabethan mansions, are a good example of this. In these gardens, bedding plants were regimented into intricately symmetrical formal patterns derived from the engraved ornament books and intricate embroidery patterns of the period. Sometimes, if plant material proved too recalcitrant to serve the gardener's purpose, colored gravel was used instead. On other occasions, the regimented patterns were made to serve a secondary, practical purpose and the different plots were planted with contrasting textures of medicinal and culinary herbs and vegetables. The subordination of nature to man was emphasized by

August **MACKE**
Garden with Pool
(detail)
1912

Ian **GARDNER**
Levens Hall
(detail)
1973

the clipping of suitable trees, such as box, into fanciful shapes: strict geometrical forms, or representations of birds and animals. The art of topiary continues to flourish today.

The above methods of gardening were derived from the idea that the garden was essentially an extension of, and therefore subordinate to, the house. After gardens ceased to be totally enclosed, and began to stretch out into the surrounding countryside, the impulse toward symmetry remained. The famous gardens of the late Renaissance in Italy—those of the Villa Lante at Bagnaia (begun in 1564), the Villa Farnese at Caprarola (completed in 1587), and the Villa d'Este at Tivoli (1550)—demonstrate human dominance over nature. Great emphasis is placed on architectural adornments, such as small pavilions, statues, and fountains. Part of the inspiration for

Vincent
VAN GOGH
The Asylum Garden
(detail)
1889

this came from the great garden built by the Roman emperor Hadrian (AD 117–138), which is also found at Tivoli. In this, Hadrian attempted to recreate some of the major wonders he had seen during his many travels.

Alfred
PARSONS
Pond in the Garden of Raku-Raku-Tei, Hikone
(detail)
c. 1900

Hadrian's garden has some curious affinities with Japanese temple gardens. These also attempt to recreate celebrated beauty spots on a reduced scale. One curious feature of these gardens is the substitution of materials—raked sand for water is the most obvious example. In Japan, reduction of scale has been carried to an extreme with the creation of miniature gardens in shallow dishes or trays. These feature bonsai, or deliberately dwarfed, trees that are trained into unusual shapes. The first record of these in Japan appears in a scroll dated 1309, but the idea was originally from China.

Ernest Arthur
ROWE
The East Court, Montacute House
(detail)
c. 1900

The minuscule Japanese gardens form a striking contrast to the great parterres created by André Le Nôtre (1613–1700) for Louis XIV at Versailles. However, the underlying principle for both these gardens, as well as Italian Renaissance gardens, is the same. A garden is viewed as essentially being a picture, something to be contemplated. Formed from a wide variety of materials, the garden still remains subject to the demands of the human creative impulse. Rather than celebrating nature itself, it really celebrates the subjection of nature to the disciplines of the esthetic impulse, which imposes a particular vision. However, Le Nôtre's garden plans have one major difference from earlier gardens. By concealing boundaries, they suggest that the amount of land at the gardener's disposal is infinite. Versailles, for example, is meant to suggest the limitless power of Louis XIV, the Sun King.

Mother and Children in a Garden, Chinese c. 1850

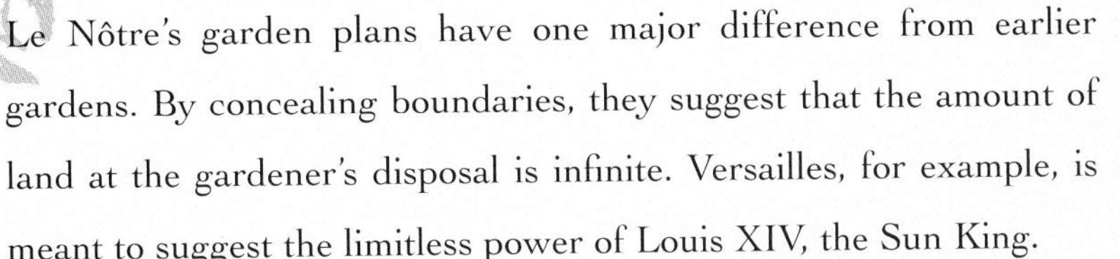

Thomas **ROBINS**
The Vegetable Garden at Charlton Park (detail)
Mid-18th century

Before the revolution of taste that was initiated by "Capability" Brown, English gardens were strictly regimented. Here, a vegetable garden divided into rectangular plots adjoins a small formal garden with a pool in its center.

August **MACKE**
Garden with Pool
1912

The German Expressionist Macke (1887–1914) depicts a garden in Edwardian style with a rectangular pool and clipped box hedges. In the background is a wire dome with creepers trained over it. The boldness of his brushwork contrasts with the formality of the layout.

Chris **BROUGHTON**
Overview, Levens Hall, Cumbria
1995

Levens Hall is Elizabethan, but the garden surrounding it dates from the early eighteenth century. This garden is perhaps the most complete surviving English formal garden dating from before "Capability" Brown and his peers who changed the look of English gardens. Though the layout is formal, it is not symmetrical. The famous topiary garden offers a random selection of different geometrical shapes. Chris Broughton (b. 1949) has always loved the garden at Levens and made this elaborate drawing in response to the recent improvements and additions that have been made to it.

Dreams and the light imaginings of men,
And all that faith creates or love desires,
Terrible, strange, sublime
and beauteous shapes.

”

PERCY BYSSHE SHELLEY (1792–1822)

Ian **GARDNER**
Levens Hall
1973

This is a close-up view of one of the clipped yew trees at Levens, which has been shaped into a spiral form that would never be seen in nature. The artist has used a traditional English watercolor technique, where transparent washes are carefully layered one over another.

Larry **SMART**
The Gardener
1986

In addition to being clipped into formal, geometrical shapes, yews and box trees are sometimes clipped into the shape of animals and birds. Here, the fact that the trees are in tubs suggests that the intention may be to move these exotic forms to a more sheltered position for the winter months.

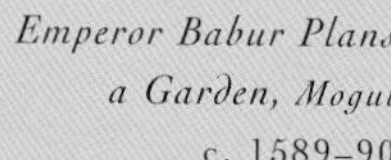

Emperor Babur Plans a Garden, Mogul
c. 1589–90

Babur, the first Mogul Emperor (1483–1530), was famous for his love of gardens. In this illustration to his "Memoirs," painted a couple of generations after his death, he is seen working with his architect (who stands facing him, holding a plan) on a new garden near Jalabad in India. The garden is typically Iranian or Indian in plan, with runnels of water dividing the space into rectangles. Versions of the same sort of design can also be found on Persian carpets.

Vincent **VAN GOGH**
The Asylum Garden
1889

The pictured asylum was at Saint-Rémy-en-Provence, near Arles and Van Gogh was confined there at his own request, early in 1889. He painted prolifically during his stay there, trying to make his painting calmer than it had been in the preceding months. This view of the asylum's courtyard, with its formal beds surrounding a circular pool, is one of the most important artistic products of his stay, which lasted for twelve months. The almost bare branches of the trees show that the picture was painted in early spring.

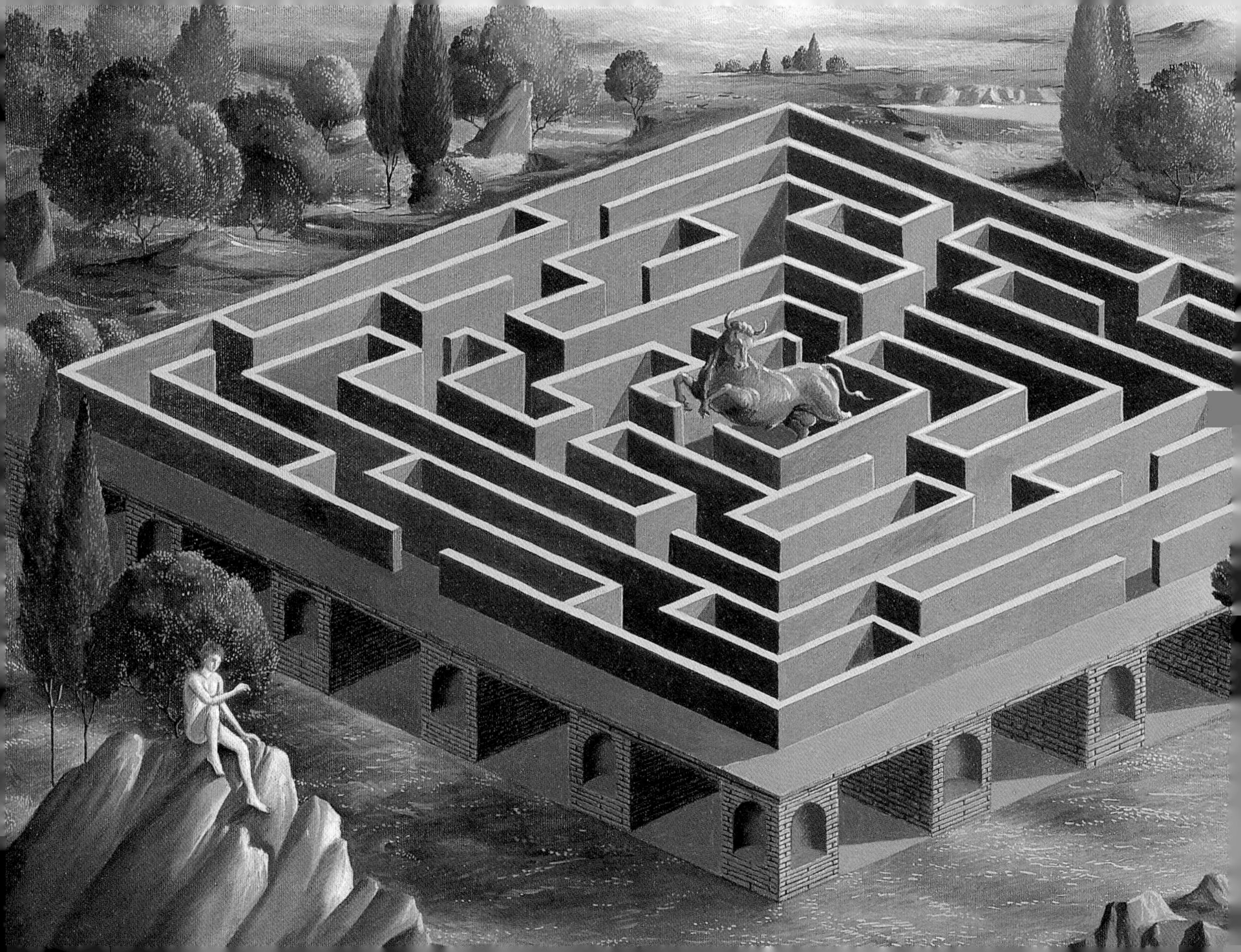

"

... At length the finish'd garden to the view
Its vistas opens, and its alleys green.
Snatch'd thro' the verdant maze, the hurried eye
Distracted wanders...

"

JAMES THOMSON (1700–48)

Salvo **RUSSO**
Lasimisio
1989

The contemporary Italian artist Salvo Russo (b.1954) offers here a visionary version of the mazes that often form part of large formal gardens. The maze is made of clipped yew hedges, within a retaining wall. At its center a statue of a bull alludes to the legend of the Minotaur—the man-bull whom the Greek hero Theseus found and slew in the labyrinth at Knossos in Crete. Some of the earliest maze designs appear on Cretan coins.

Stefano **DI STASIO**
Dangerous Reading
1987

Absorbed in his book, the figure stands in a symbolic trench; the implication is that he has scarred the ground—i.e. nature—merely by walking. Above him hover what seem to be instruments of torture, among them the wheel associated with St. Catherine. The setting is a neat avenue of trees of a kind that are in keeping with formal garden layouts on a large scale, but the protagonist ignores the direction that they suggest.

“*A garden must be looked unto and dressed as the body*”

HERBERT (1640)

Mother and Children in a Garden, Chinese
c. 1850

This painting is typical of those produced in China for the European market during the mid-nineteenth century; it adopts European perspective and conventions. The garden itself remains typically Chinese, with paved terraces, specimen plants in pots, and small pavilions. Each of these pavilions provided a point of rest from which to admire a different, carefully framed view.

◀ *previous page*

Alfred **PARSONS**
Pond in the Garden of Raku-Raku-Tei, Hikone
c. 1900

Hikone stands on the shores of Lake Biwa in Japan, which is famous both for the beauty of its scenery and its cultured pearls. It has long been a tourist center. This painting is a late Victorian or early Edwardian rendition of a typical Japanese garden, and it includes appropriately costumed figures in the distance. The resolutely European technique emphasizes the close resemblance to Monet's (1840–1926) famous garden at Giverny.

Lithian **RICCI**
Roman Gardens at the Villa Medici
1988

The Villa Medici was built in 1574–80 and, although originally a Medici possession, it is now the headquarters of the French Academy in Rome. Lithian Ricci has had the witty idea of framing a view of its garden with screens where other, miniature garden views appear. To the right stands a mythological monster, in the manner of Arcimboldo (*see page 272*), with a body entirely composed of various flowers.

Lithian **RICCI**
In the Heart of the Garden
1996

The artist offers the viewer a visual pun; a female figure, herself, gives a symbolic heart to a male companion. Both figures are seated on flowery thrones in the midst of a typical Italian garden, with flights of steps, clipped hedges, and fountains. Just visible in the foreground is a garden plan, which suggests that the garden consists of concentric areas, and the figures are seated near the very middle, or "heart," of it, which is represented by the fountain directly behind them.

Ernest Arthur
ROWE
Campsea Ashe, Suffolk
c. 1900

This watercolor shows a late Victorian attempt to combine the formality of a topiary garden, like that at Levens Hall, with the kind of lavish planting that had come into fashion. The clipped hedges shelter beds crammed with flowers, with tall hollyhocks conspicuous among them.

David **LIGARE**
Still Life with Roses and Arrow
1999

The American artist David Ligare (b. 1945) was inspired here by the countryside near Salinas, California, which is where he lives. He contrasts the flowers, now confined in their vase, with the sweeping countryside beyond the window ledge. The arrow is an emblem of the sun-god Apollo, the deity who presides over the whole panorama.

Engraving after
Jacques **RIGAUD**
The Domes in the Garden at Versailles
1794

Published at the height of the French Revolution (the Terror, led by Robespierre, did not finish until the end of July 1794), this engraving commemorates the splendor of the gardens of the royal chateau as they appeared during the reign of Louis XV. As in somewhat earlier Italian gardens, the elements of symmetry and formality continue to be stressed.

Arthur **MELVILLE**
The Italian Garden
c. 1870

An "Italianate" style, derived from late Renaissance building, flourished in England in the mid-nineteenth century, as an alternative to Gothic style. Italian patterns were also favored for gardens, though they were usually adorned, as here, with masses of flowering plants that had had no place in the Italian originals.

God Almighty first planted a garden... It is the greatest Refreshment to the Spirits of Man; without which, Buildings and Palaces are but gross handyworks.

”

FRANCIS BACON (1561–1626)

Lithograph after Albert **TOLLER**
Ornamental Garden of a Suburban Villa
c. 1880

This lithograph demonstrates how variants of the nineteenth-century Italianate style in gardening spread right across Europe. It was successful in becoming one of the trappings of bourgeois pretentiousness.

Ernest Arthur **ROWE**
The East Court, Montacute House
c. 1900

Montacute House in Somerset, England, built between 1588 and 1601, is an outstanding example of Elizabethan architecture's rather wayward use of classical motifs. At the time that this watercolor was painted, the house had recently been bought and restored by Lord Curzon (1859–1925), who was appointed Viceroy of India in 1898 and Foreign Secretary after World War I. The garden shows all of Curzon's sense of lavishness, with herbaceous borders inspired by the garden designer Gertrude Jekyll (1843–1942).

Luigi **BAZZANI**
In a Courtyard in Pompeii
c. 1900

Somewhat in the manner of Alma-Tadema (*see pages 144-5*), this shows an Italian artist of the late nineteenth century attempting to imagine how his forbears might have lived in Pompeii, the Roman city fourteen miles south-east of Naples, which was overwhelmed by an eruption of Vesuvius in AD 79.

F. Scott **HESS**
The Night Gardener's Escape
1995

Elements from the Italianate tradition can be seen here; the row of ilexes in the background are used to conjure up a sinister atmosphere, reinforced by the anguished expression on the face.

Jean-Baptiste **COROT**
The Gardens of the Villa d'Este, Tivoli
1843

Rather typically, Corot (1796–1875) elects to show only a detail of the garden itself. Instead, the spectator is invited to look beyond to the picturesquely jumbled town buildings.

Roberto **MARQUEZ**
Nude Ascending a Staircase
1999

The painting is intended as a retort to Marcel Duchamp's (1887–1968) famous *Nude Descending a Staircase* (1912), one of the icons of the Modern Movement. Marquez (b. 1959) shows his nude hemmed in by severe figures in monks' robes, one of whom turns his head to stare disapprovingly at the nude figure.

Robert **BISSELL**
Runaround
1996

The clipped hedge here is an unnatural hue close to blood-red. It separates two natural antagonists; the black dog running round its perimeter, and the alert and slightly complacent rabbit sheltering within it.

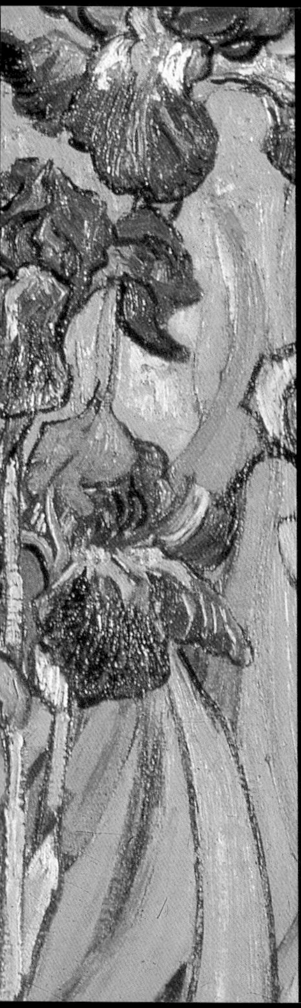

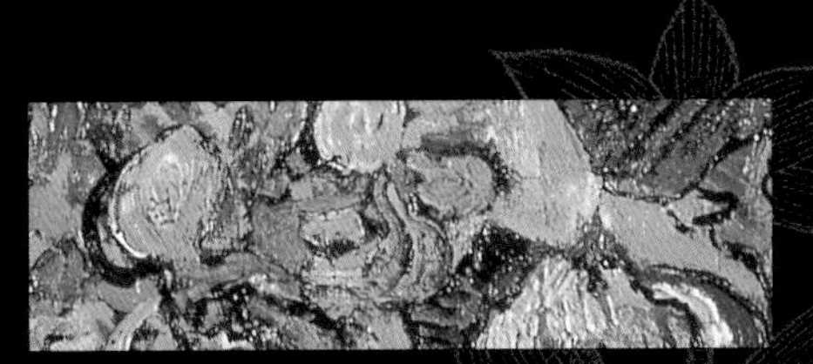

CHAPTER FOUR

collectors' passion

"Bare flowers, that I could gallant it like you
And be as little vaine,
You come abroad, and make a harmless shew,
And to your beds of Earthe again"

HENRY KING (1592—1669)

Vincent **VAN GOGH**
Iris
(detail)
1891

THE APPEARANCE OF GARDENS has been altered constantly throughout the centuries. This has been due to the introduction of new plants and, by selective breeding, the alteration of those already well-known. New species of plant were being traded across long distances as early as Roman times. And gardeners were, even then, trying to change the colors of flowers and increase the length of their flowering season by selective cross-breeding.

Hunt SLONEM
Catelaya
(detail)
1991

The passion for the strange and the rare was embodied by the collectors' cabinets put together by aristocratic Renaissance collectors. The most striking manifestation of this passion was the "tulipmania" that swept the Netherlands during the eighteenth century. Bulbs of ornamental tulips became the subject of feverish financial speculation until the market finally collapsed, leaving many of the speculators ruined. During this fevered

Charles
CURRAN
Chrysanthemums
(detail)
1890

time, artists were employed to compile tulip-books, recording the most desired colors and varieties. A rather similar passion for rare orchids flourished among the nouveaux riches at the turn of the twentieth century. These plants—rare, difficult to cultivate, and often from exotic locations—became symbols of prestige and also, to some extent at least, symbols of the decadent lifestyle of the *fin-de-siècle*.

Katushika
HOKUSAI
The Eightfold Bridges
1831–2

One intriguing aspect of plant collecting was the passion for the monstrous and seemingly freakish. Plants were cultivated not for their beauty, but for their symbolic value—certain fungi and cacti, for instance, aroused curiosity because of their phallic appearance. The mandrake, with its forked root, was thought to resemble the figure of a man. It was said that the plant shrieked when pulled from the ground, and that this sound killed or drove mad those who did not block their ears against it. The only safe way of uprooting a mandrake was to do it by moonlight, using a black dog attached to the plant by a cord. Human hands were not supposed to come into contact with it. Once the plant had been dragged from the earth; it could be used as a love charm, as a soporific, or to induce pregnancy.

James
COLLINSON
The Garden Boy
(detail)
date unknown

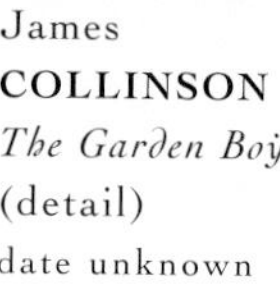

Gathering the Fruit of the Mandrake
Early 15th century

The mandrake is a good example of a plant whose fame was based on a kind of anthropomorphism. Before the birth of true science, theories concerning the properties of plants were based largely on their outward appearances. The good or harm a particular plant could produce was something deduced, not from controlled experimentation, but from the appearance of the plant itself, which, it was believed, sent a signal concerning its usefulness or harmfulness to humankind. This view prevailed worldwide, even in cultures like that of China, which did not see humans as the center and focus of the universe. Indeed to this day, Chinese traditional medicine often selects herbs and plants according to their appearances. Within this viewpoint, the whole world was perceived as a system of occult correspondences, and the adept could attune himself or herself to these, for both good and evil purposes. The gardener and the witch were not so far apart...

The rational classification of plants, according to their genera, did not really get under way until the work of the great Swedish botanist Carl Linnaeus (1707–78) was published; *Systema Naturae* in 1735, and *Species Plantarum* in 1753. Though Linnaeus was not a citizen of one of the great colonial powers, part of the impetus behind his work was supplied by the discoveries that were being made during the age of exploration, powered by the colonizing impulse.

Pierre-Auguste
RENOIR
The Conservatory
(detail)
1864

Martin **JOHNSON HEADE**
An Orchid with a Pair of Hummingbirds
c. 1890s

American art was relatively slow to develop ways of dealing with natural phenomena that lay outside the usual range of European experience. Martin Johnson Heade's (1819–1904) close-up views of orchids in tropical settings give the full impact of the exoticism and rarity of these blooms. These are near-photographic close-ups, made before photography invented them.

Hunt **SLONEM**
Catelaya
1991

This portrait of a rare orchid in a gilt frame offers a good rendering of the slightly sinister sexiness of many of these plants. There are an enormous number of different species—botanical authorities estimate the number at around 35,000. Speaking of sexiness, the word "orchid" derives from the Ancient Greek for "testicle"—though this refers to the shape of the tuber, not the flower.

Henry **WALLIS**
Corner of an Eastern Courtyard
19th century

This may have been a detail painted as an aide-mémoire for a more ambitious composition. Alternatively, it may be an oil sketch made for its own sake, simply for the artist's pleasure. Many leading Victorian painters produced these, Lord Leighton (1830–96) among them. A painting of this kind would not have been considered salable in Victorian times because of its lack of a specific subject, but informal sketches of this type are eagerly collected today.

"*I love all that thou lovest,*
Spirit of Delight:
The fresh earth in new leaves dressed,
And the starry night."

PERCY BYSSHE SHELLEY (1792–1822)

F. Scott **HESS**
Her Garden
1990

Hess (b. 1955) finds the sensual aspect in everyday situations. Here, the succulents and cactus plants are fleshy and suggest sexual innuendoes as the woman fondles her plants, all the while observing the body of her gardener.

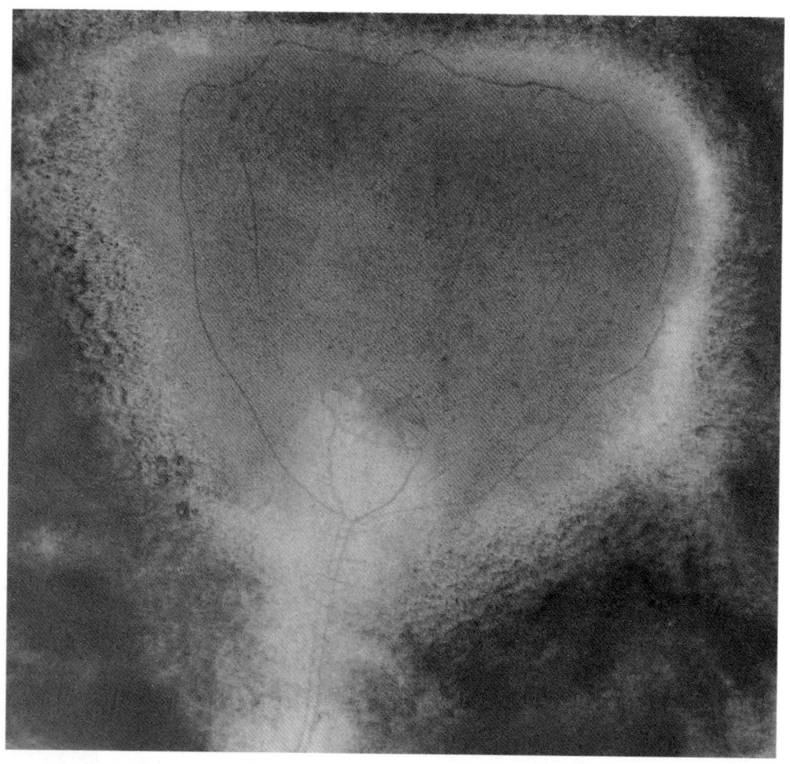

David **WILLETS**
The Poppy Fields
1999

This is a near-abstract image derived from the artist's close examination of the natural cycles of plants. Both the ephemeral bloom of the poppy and the seed-head that appears when the petals fall are ghostlike presences here.

Pierre-Auguste **RENOIR**
The Conservatory
1864

Of all the Impressionist artists, Renoir (1841–1919) is the one who seems to have felt the greatest attraction to the life of the new rich of his time. This is understandable, since he was the one who came from the poorest background. This composition documents an ambitious bourgeois garden, filled with a collection of the sprawling tea-roses so popular at the time and equipped—a sure sign of luxury—with a large hothouse for more tender blooms.

> *Sweet as the primrose peeps beneath the thorn*

OLIVER GOLDSMITH (1728–74)

Lesley **FOTHERBY**
Primulas in a Greenhouse (detail)
20th century

Primulas, also called primroses, appeal to plant collectors because of their compactness and wide variety of colors. Those usually grown in greenhouses include the Fairy Primrose (*Primula malacoides*) and the Chinese Primrose (*Primula sinensis*). Many other varieties are popular as outdoor plants.

Katushika **HOKUSAI**
The Eightfold Bridges
1831–32

The Japanese liked to collect nature in situ. Series of prints by both Hokusai (1760–1849) and Hiroshige (1797–1858) record famous beauty spots. Tourists were encouraged to match their viewing position as closely as possible to that of the artist's.

Kitagawa **UTAMARO**
Scene 1, Comparison of celebrated beauties and the Loyal League
c. 1797

A typically allusive composition by one of the great masters of the Japanese print. The comparison proposed is presumably between the two sumptuously arrayed geishas to the left and the figures in the background. The kneeling female figure in the back right is a maiko, or apprentice. In the center of the composition, as a token of refinement, stands a miniature garden on a tray, with two bonsai—a dwarf pine tree and a dwarf cherry. Bonsai have now become much coveted collectors' objects in the West as well as in Japan.

> *Buttercups and daises, oh, the pretty flowers,*
> *Coming ere the Springtime to tell of sunny hours.*

MARY HOWITT (1799–1888)

Jane **LOUDON**
Forget-me-nots and Buttercups
1842

This is a plate from *The Ladies' Flower Garden,* which is one example of the illustrated albums specifically addressed to a female audience that were immensely popular in Victorian times. They were probably given as presents by male admirers. The flowers included in such works seem to have been chosen largely for their sentimental connotations.

Chu Hing **WAH**
Three Pots of Color
1996

The contemporary Chinese watercolorist Chu Hing Wah lives and works in Hong Kong. His paintings are a mixture of modern and traditional techniques. Here he illustrates the Chinese preference for displaying plants separately, in pots, instead of mixing them together in a flower bed.

Gathering the Fruit of the Mandrake,
Early 15th century

An illustration for a *Notebook on Health* that seems to demonstrate that the mandrake, at this time, remained a largely legendary commodity. In general, it was the root not the fruit that was sought.

"

Go and catch a falling star,
Get with child a mandrake root,
Tell me, where all past years are,
Or who cleft the Devil's foot.

"

JOHN DONNE (c. 1571–1631)

And 'tis my faith that
Every flower
Enjoys the air it breathes

WILLIAM WORDSWORTH (1770–1850)

Dorothy **HENRIQUES WELLS**
Wild Banana
1996

This watercolor of a Bird of Paradise plant portrays an ornamental species often seen in Jamaican gardens. It is so-named because of a fancied resemblance to the brilliantly plumed birds of paradise that inhabit the jungles of New Guinea, as well as the island of Little Tobago, off the coast of Trinidad in the West Indies.

Charles **CURRAN**
Chrysanthemums
1890

Chrysanthemums became fashionable with the wave of enthusiasm for all things Japanese that began in Europe in the mid-nineteenth century, when Japan was finally opened to European trade. This trend continued into the early years of the twentieth century.

> "*Presently they came to the long glittering range of greenhouses and hot-houses.*"
>
> **ELIZABETH GASKELL** (1810–65)

James **COLLINSON**
The Garden Boy
date unknown

This delightful watercolor hints at how fashionable the cult of gardening became in Victorian England. The boy, given his occupation, is very smartly dressed, and he carries a precious pot plant in each hand with an air of confidence. The plants are a tree peony (*Paeonia suffruticosa*) and an *Abutilon vitifolium*, both plants that Victorians would have housed in a conservatory.

Marianne **ARNBACK**
Spiral Plants
1996

The forms here clearly derive from fern fronds, but the artist imbues them with mystical significance. She describes her work as "painting a window into nature." Natural forms here preside over a marriage between fantasy and reality.

David **BLAIR**
Hare's Foot Fern
c. 1880

This is a plate from one of the great color books of botanical illustrations, *European Ferns*, which were a characteristic enterprise of the nineteenth century. Both professional botanists and amateurs took pleasure in classifying all the differe plant species.

"

Not God! in gardens! when the eve is cool?

Nay, but I have a sign,

'Tis very sure God walks in mine.

"

THOMAS EDWARD BROWN (1830–97)

Alfred **PARSONS**

A Garden near the Thames

date unknown

This watercolor represents faithfully the typical late Victorian and early Edwardian method of planting. The wild profusion of different flower varieties, such as delphiniums, irises, and lavender, echoed the geographical extent of the British Empire itself.

John **NAVA**
Still Life with Parrot and French Tulips
1999

This attractive, realist still life portrays tulips of the kind that can now be bought at any florist. They are nevertheless very similar to the varieties that were so fiercely collected in the early eighteenth century during the height of "tulipmania."

The Queen of bulbous plants,
whose flower is beautiful
in its figure, and most rich
and admirable in color.

”

SIR THOMAS HAMMER (1712–1769)

Barbara **DIETZSCH**
Parrot Tulip with Butterfly and Beetle
c. 1750

Though a little later than the period of "tulipmania," this album leaf is still a good example of the portraits of tulips that were made at that time. Striped varieties were especially highly valued.

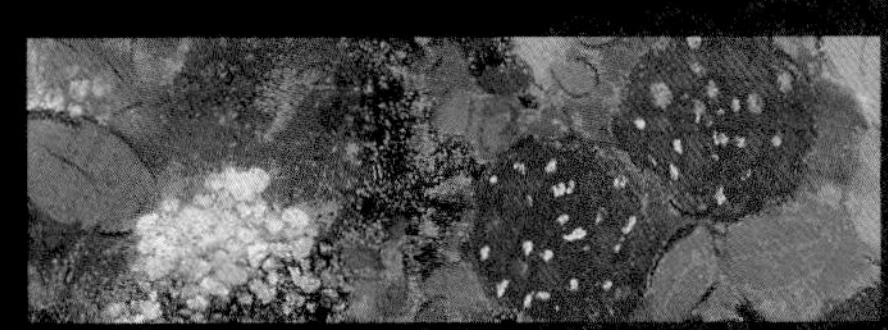

CHAPTER FIVE

the language of flowe

"Through breaks of the
cedar and sycamore bowers
Struggles the light
that is love to the flowers..."

HENRY CLARENCE KENDALL (1839–82)

Odilon **REDON**
Ophelia Among the Flowers
(detail)
c. 1905–8

DURING THE NINETEENTH CENTURY there was a fashion for attractive little books that supposedly illustrated "the language of flowers." With the help of these, young men could send bouquets to the young women of their choice, spelling out precisely nuanced sentimental messages. In fact, flower symbolism had a much longer and more complex history than the compilers of these books realized. In the Greek and Roman world, for example, flowers were symbolic not because of their particular species, but because they were all ephemeral, and they spoke of the transitoriness of life. It was for this reason that people wore them as garlands at banquets, and also strewed them on the bodies of the dead before cremation.

Ghisbert
COMBAZ
The Bouquet
(detail)
c. 1912

Flowers placed in the Dutch still-life paintings of the seventeenth century, especially those scattered on a

Sir Lawrence **ALMA-TADEMA**
Ask Me No More
(detail)
1906

surface, had the same kind of significance—the ephemerality of life—as they possessed in the Greek and Roman world. But they also often had another kind of symbolism as well. Paintings of this period, both Dutch and Italian, were often produced in sets, emblematic of the five senses. Flowers were used to symbolize the sense of smell.

Some species of flowers have had absolutely specific symbolic meanings attached to them. Lilies are emblems of purity and are therefore often shown in paintings of the Virgin—a vase of lilies is a frequent addition to depictions of the Annunciation. A pink or carnation was an emblem of impending marriage and, in sixteenth- and seventeenth-century marriage portraits, a man is frequently shown holding this flower as a sign of his betrothal. A sunflower

Alberto **ABATE**
Vitalia
(detail)
1993

sometimes served as an emblem of royal favor. It plays this role in the best known of Van Dyck's (1599–1641) self-portraits, in which the artist also displays a gold chain given to him by his patron Charles I.

Marc **CHAGALL**
The Bride with Flowers
(detail)
1960

The symbolism of plants, flowers, and fruits is even more complex in Oriental art than it is in Western art. Almost everything that grows has its own significance in this art. In Japan, the bamboo is one of the three trees of good omen (together with the pine and the plum). In China it is admired for its straightness, which is seen as a symbol of integrity. For some Buddhist Masters, the rustle of bamboo is the signal for enlightenment. One celebrated Chinese monk, however, achieved his own enlightenment through the contemplation of peach blossom. In Japan this blossom is a symbol of

Eleanor **FORTESCUE-BRICKDALE**
If I Could Have That Little Head
c. 1909

virginity, much as the lily is in the West. The fruit of the peach is, on the other hand, also one of the Chinese emblems of immortality, and it is regarded as the food of the Immortals.

One result of the intricate alliance of different symbolisms is that almost every representation of nature to be found in classic Chinese or Japanese art has a subtext that an initiated audience was expected to be able to construe easily. It is not just the individual objects depicted that convey a message—the message is reinforced by the presence of apparently unrelated items. In Chinese porcelain, peaches are often combined with bats (emblems of longevity because they live in caves, which are entrances to the realm of the Immortals). The whole design became a wish for good fortune in the New Year, when these porcelains were offered as gifts.

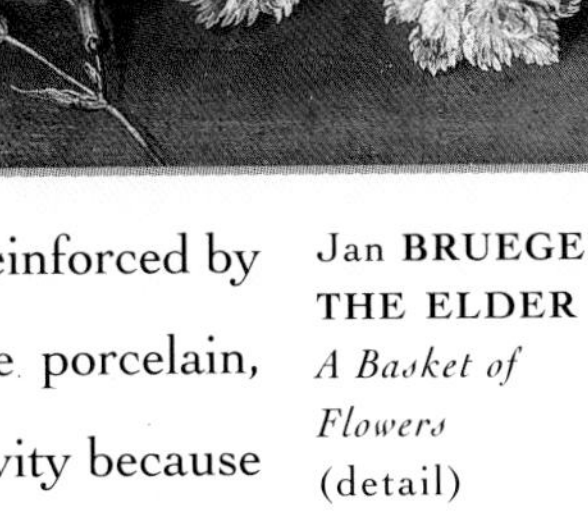

Jan **BRUEGEL THE ELDER**
A Basket of Flowers
(detail)
Early 17th century

> *I must not say that thou wast true*
> *Yet let me say that thou wast fair;*
> *And they, that lovely face that view,*
> *Why should they ask if truth be there?*

MATTHEW ARNOLD (1822–88)

Sir Lawrence **ALMA-TADEMA**
Ask Me No More
1906

The bouquet of flowers tied with a ribbon and lying on the marble bench here plays its traditional role as a lover's gift. The title of the painting suggests a degree of resistance on the part of the lady—it is in fact a misapplied line from a famous lyric by Thomas Carew (1594–1639/40): "Ask me no more where Jove bestows/When June is past the fading rose..."

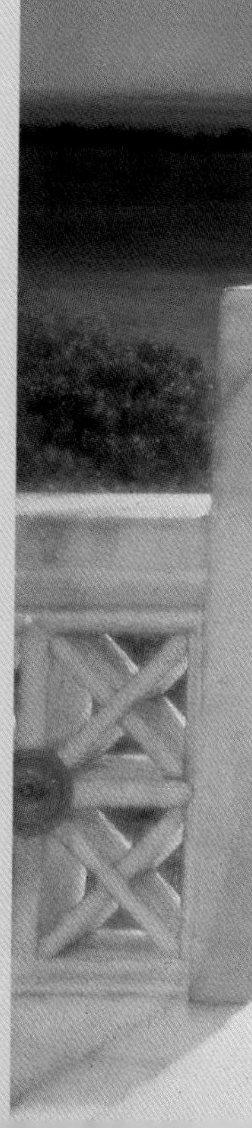

Gina Marie
BERNARDINI
Bliss (detail)
1950s

The ecstasy of a lesbian embrace finds an emblem in the bunch of white daisies that one partner presents to the other. The Expressionist style reinforces the emotional content of the painting.

Marc **CHAGALL**
The Bride with Flowers
1960

In this late gouache, Chagall (1887–1985) uses one of his favorite motifs—the bride who floats ecstatically in the heavens. She was originally an emblem of his love for his first wife, Bella. The flowers that surround her resolve themselves, upon close inspection, into the heads of the lovers kissing.

Alberto **ABATE**
Vitalia
1993

Abate's compositions often look back to the world of Symbolism. His *Vitalia*, holding a single lily and a peacock feather, is the descendant of the mysterious "femmes fatales" painted by the French Symbolist Gustave Moreau (1826–98).

Édouard **MANET**
Olympia
1863

The offense caused by this picture when it was first exhibited is closely linked to the bouquet presented by the black servant. This suggests that the main figure is a courtesan receiving a tribute from an admirer.

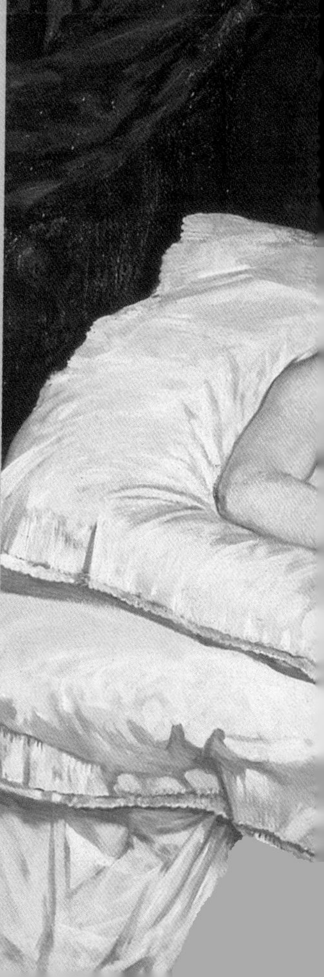

For this most goodly flower

So Jupiter me succour,

She flourisheth new and new

In beauty and virtue.

”

JOHN SKELTON (c. 1460–1529)

After Henri **LAFON**
The Bride
1852–3

In this mid-nineteenth century print the bride of the title carries the traditional sprig of orange blossom close to her breast. Her bouquet of white roses, symbolic of purity, spills from a florist's box on the floor.

Anonymous greeting card
Pinning the Boutonnière
c. 1900

A woman places a flower in the buttonhole of her companion. This intimate gesture combines love with more than a touch of possessiveness. The roses flowering around them indicate their emotional state.

Jan Van **HUYSUM**
Flowers in a Terracotta Vase
1744

Van Huysum's (1682–1749) paintings stand at the end of the long development of the Dutch flower-piece. A painting of this sort was intended to symbolize the careless abundance of nature, even though the flowers themselves were carefully painted from separate studies.

Jan **BRUEGEL THE ELDER**
A Basket of Flowers
Early 17th century

Jan Bruegel (1568–1625) painted few pure flower-pieces. As with the Van Huysum opposite, the individual blooms were meticulously painted using studies made from nature. The message, once again, concerns the abundance of the natural world.

Sir Lawrence **ALMA-TADEMA**

When Flowers Return

date unknown

Fresher and more spontaneous in treatment than Alma-Tadema's (1836–1912) usual style, this painting celebrates the return of spring by entwining two female figures with a garland of daffodils.

Dante Gabriel **ROSSETTI**

Venus Verticordia

1864–8

An early example of the opulent female half-lengths that became a specialty of the artist, this painting shows the goddess as a pagan version of a Christian martyr, equipped with a halo and pointing an arrow toward her own breast. The opulent roses that surround her are floral equivalents of her own beauty.

Elsie **BUNGE**
Woman with White Magnolias (detail)
1950s

Influenced by the work of Matisse (1869–1954), this Argentinian artist uses a bouquet of white blooms as an emblem of simplicity. Though the picture was painted in the 1950s, it also shows the influence of the Deco style, which had an enduring success in Latin America.

“
To lose the touch of flowers...
is the supreme separation.
”

ALBERT CAMUS (1913–60)

Ghisbert **COMBAZ**
The Bouquet
c. 1912

The woman, contemplating a large bunch of roses, is dressed in a style made fashionable just before World War I by the couturier Paul Poiret (1879–1944). Poiret combined a revival of the Empire style of the early nineteenth century with details, especially colors, borrowed from the Ballet Russe, which was then having a triumphant success in Paris.

Sir Lawrence
ALMA-TADEMA
A Roman Garden
1878

This relatively early work by Alma-Tadema (1836–1912) shows an anguished woman embracing a child. The poppies, roses and sunflowers in the garden seem to speak of death and immortality.

Lily **SALVO**
The Gate of Desire
1998

This painting presents a gigantic rose as the gateway to a world of dream. Contemplating the flower, the dreamer pictured enters into a new realm.

Stefano di **STASIO**
Happy Hours
1996

The subject is a visionary or dreamer standing at an open window. A garland of roses traverses the night sky and, entering by another window behind him, begins to entwine his bed. A similar garland is wound round his forearm. The story therefore seems to be one of love fulfilled or soon to be fulfilled.

QUING DYNASTY

Peach Blossom

19th century

The fruit of the peach was one of the Chinese emblems of longevity, but in this drawing the blossom is simply there for its own sake. The sharply focused realistic technique indicates that it was actually intended for a European customer rather than a Chinese one.

ICHIMYOSAI

Bee and Peony

19th century

This image is painted in a style that originated in China with the "bird and flower" paintings of the Emperor Hui Tsung (reigned 1100–1125). The peony, called "the king of flowers" by the Chinese, traditionally symbolized good fortune.

Lithian **RICCI**
Son of Flowers
1998

The Arcimboldoesque figure of a child made entirely of flowers is held suspended by two crowned figures over a stream. The background is provided by a painting-within-a-painting – a depiction of Niagara – and huge raindrops or teardrops run down the walls. The elements in this picture combine to form an allegory of fertility.

"

You are a garden locked up,

my sister, my bride;...

Your plants are an orchard of

pomegranates with choice fruits.

"

SONG OF SONGS 4:12–13

Joseph-Marie **VIEN**
Greek Youth Crowning
His Beloved with Flowers
1773

Vien (1716–1809) was one of the pioneers of the Neoclassical movement in France. The youth crowning his beloved symbolizes aspirations towards naturalness and simplicity. The image is inspired by the writings of the philosopher and novelist Jean-Jacques Rousseau (1712–78).

Benozzo **GOZZOLI**
Angel Gathering Flowers in a Heavenly Landscape
c. 1460

One of the most poetic of all images of Paradise, this Florentine Renaissance painting of angels gathering roses sums up the Christian idea of heavenly bliss. The flowers have been specifically chosen because they are intimately associated with the Virgin.

Nymphenburg Porcelain
c. 1760–6

This detail is from a table service made for the court of the Elector of Bavaria, the patron of the Nymphenburg porcelain factory. The softly modeled tulips and roses were influenced by the work of painters like Jan Van Huysum (*see page 152*).

Stefania **FABRIZI**
Rose of the Desert
1995

Another version of the idea expressed by Lily Salvo in *The Gate of Desire* (*see page 160*). The desert rose is the symbol of improbable or unlooked-for perfection, springing from apparently barren soil.

Sir Lawrence
ALMA-TADEMA
The Roses of Heliogabalus
1888

One of Alma-Tadema's (1836–1912) most celebrated works, this refers to the legend of the decadent Roman Emperor Heliogabalus (ruled AD 218–222) who is said to have smothered his dinner guests with the sheer weight of the rose petals that were showered upon them.

John Atkinson **GRIMSHAW**
The Rector's Garden, Queen of the Lilies
1877

The white dress of the girl and the stem of white lilies she is holding combine to make a statement about female purity. Similar lilies feature in numerous religious paintings depicting the Annunciation, and the artist clearly drew on this tradition.

Thomas Falcon **MARSHALL**
May Day Garlands
1873

May 1 has long been the traditional day for holding springtime celebrations. This probably dates from pre-Christian times and may still incorporate traces of pagan rituals. Green branches and floral garlands, carried in procession, form part of the rituals meant to ensure fertility.

"

There is a garden in her face,
Where roses and white lilies grow;
A heav'nly paradise is that place,
Wherein all pleasant fruits do flow.
There cherries grow, which none
may buy…

Those cherries fairly do enclose
of orient pearl a double row;
Which when her lovely laughter show,
They look like rosebuds fill'd
with snow.

"

THOMAS CAMPION (1567–1620)

Eleanor **FORTESCUE-BRICKDALE**
If I Could Have That Little Head
c. 1909

A profile portrait in a style borrowed from fifteenth-century Italy. A pink or carnation included in such a portrait generally signified that it was painted to celebrate a betrothal. But in fifteenth- and sixteenth-century paintings the flower is usually held by a man.

Giovanni Battista **SALVI**
called **SASSOFERATO**
Madonna
Mid-17th century

Sassoferato's (1609–85) work reflects the pious atmosphere of seventeenth-century Rome. The custom of surrounding images of the Madonna with wreaths of flowers as an allusion to the subject's beauty and purity was not, however, peculiar to him, or to Rome itself. There are also similar compositions, for example, in the work of Rubens (1577–1640).

All men are like grass,
and all their glory is like the
flowers of the field;
the grass withers and the
flowers fall

”

I PETER 1:24

Ancient Egypt
The Book of the Dead
c. 1250BC

The scribe Ani and his wife appear in this funeral papyrus wearing ceremonial garlands and making offerings to the gods, which include bunches of papyrus flowers. The remains of actual garlands found in tombs show that flowers played an important part in ancient Egyptian rituals.

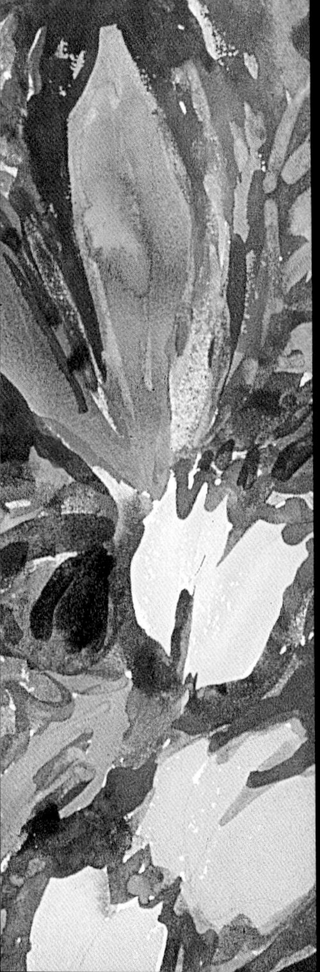

Hunt **SLONEM**
Catelayas
1992

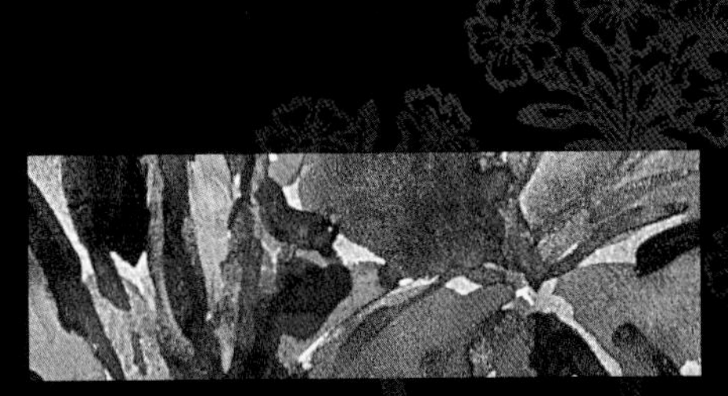

CHAPTER SIX

nature and the traveler

"...her lover's genius form'd
A glittering fane, where rare
and alien plants
Might safely flourish."

WILLIAM MASON (1795–1821)

THE EUROPEAN URGE TO TRAVEL eventually changed the look of gardens everywhere. The crusades had been an expression of their restlessness and the desire to expand—so was the great journey made by Marco Polo (1254–1324) along what was in fact an old-established caravan route to China. But it was the series of voyages that began with Columbus' (1451–1505) first sailing across the Atlantic in 1492 that really set things going. Columbus' adventure opened a whole new world to curious and fascinated Europeans and resulted in the introduction of the potato, which soon became a staple food crop in many parts of Europe. The voyages of the Portuguese mariner Vasco da Gama (c. 1460–1524) were equally influential in broadening the spectrum of plants known to, and cultivated in, European gardens.

William
HAVELL
Garden Scene on the Braganza Shore, Rio de Janeiro
(detail)
c. 1816

William
DANIELL
South-east view of the Hill Fort of Bijaigaih, Bihar
(detail)
1830s

The introduction of exotic species had a number of originally unforeseen results. Firstly, plants began to be collected for their own sake and were valued for their rarity. The same impulse inspired the collectors of exotic shells and minerals, who appeared at the same time. Secondly, gardeners began to look more closely at the climatic conditions that these new species required in order to flourish. It was one thing to grow a particular plant, but another to get it to flower, or to provide fruit. Remote jungles or deserts might not strike Europeans as the most desirable places to live, but in order to cultivate their new acquisitions successfully they had to find ways of providing the exotic plants with the kind of conditions they liked. In some cases, special buildings had to be created in order to provide plants with these preferred conditions. The first of these buildings

John Frederick
LEWIS
In the Bey's Garden
(detail)
1865

was the orangery—the earliest examples date from the sixteenth century and were fairly rough constructions made largely of planks and sacking, designed to protect orange trees from frost in latitudes that were really too cold for them. Later, orangeries became palatial buildings of the kind seen at Versailles.

Hank **PITCHER**
Point Conception
(detail)
1998

The more modest relation of the orangery was the glasshouse. As sheets of glass, for use in windows, gradually became both larger and cheaper, buildings made to shelter tender plants from the cold became lighter and more skeletal in construction. From the basic greenhouse, in turn, developed the conservatory—a structure made almost entirely of glass, which could be heated to a fully tropical temperature. These structures were

Tofat **AL-AHRAR**
Two Princesses in a Garden, Bokhara
(detail)
1568

creations of the early Victorian age. The great greenhouses built at Chatsworth in 1840 and 1850 by Sir Joseph Paxton (1801–65) for his patron, the Duke of Devonshire, were the models for the Crystal Palace, which housed the Great Exhibition of 1851. The second of Paxton's structures for the Duke was designed to shelter a specimen of the *Victoria regia* lily from South America, regarded by Victorian empire-builders as one of the floral wonders of the world. For an Englishman to cultivate it in his own country was an indication not only of vast wealth, which the Duke certainly possessed, but also served as a statement of the extent of Britain's colonial possessions. The plant had been discovered in 1835, in what was then British Guyana, by the Anglo-German explorer, Sir Robert Hermann Schomburgk (1804–65), and it remains the largest species of lily known.

Carlo
BERTOCCI
Giotto
(detail)
1989

> *But the majestic River floated on,*
> *Out of the mist and hum of that low land.*

MATTHEW ARNOLD (1822–88)

Norton **BUSH**
Tropical Haze
1879

In the closing years of the nineteenth century American landscape painters started to make a real effort to come to terms with types of scenery that were radically different from the models they found in European art. This, which seems to be a fantasy based on the Florida Everglades, is a case in point. Norton Bush gives the landscape a dreamlike quality. Works of this type were later to provide inspiration for illustrators of science fiction in the 1950s and 1960s—the image resembles some of the strange universes dreamed up by the author J.G. Ballard (b. 1930).

Hank **PITCHER**
Point Conception
1998

Pitcher lives in Santa Barbara, California, and the nearby Pacific coastline is part of his preferred subject matter. This particular image renders the grandeur and spaciousness of the coastal scenery.

William **HAVELL**
Garden Scene on the Braganza Shore, Rio de Janeiro (detail)
c. 1816

The itinerant British artist William Havell (1782–1857) visited Rio, then the capital of Brazil, during the period when the Portuguese Regent, Dom Jão (later King John VI), had taken refuge there from the Napoleonic Wars. He arrived in 1808, and did not depart until 1821, when he left his son, Dom Pedro, in charge of the country. Havell's view, made on the outskirts of Rio, reflects both the exoticism of the country, as perceived through European eyes, and its ambition to become more like Europe. The composition uses the long-established European formulae, which can also be seen in Claude's influential views of the Roman Campagna, made in the seventeenth century (*see page 215*).

> "*Who loves a Garden, loves a greenhouse too. Unconscious of a less propitious clime There blooms exotic beauty, warm and snug*"
>
> **WILLIAM COWPER** (1731–1800)

Winter Garden—print from the series "Grand Théâtre Nouveau", Epinal
c. 1880

In the eighteenth and nineteenth century the French town of Epinal became famous for its massive production of cheap colored prints, "Imageries d'Epinal." This example is a naïve representation of a tropical greenhouse, and it echoes the popular fascination with the exotic.

Frank **ROMERO**
Fiesta Palms
1992

This is an amusing three-dimensional tribute to a ubiquitous feature of the Southern California landscape. Carving the palms in wood, Romero gives them a stylized decorativeness that looks back to the eighteenth and early nineteenth centuries, when carved palm trees were often used for ornamental purposes.

Wes **CHRISTENSEN**
Eck in the New World
1994

Eck (Alec) Finlay is the son of Ian Hamilton Finlay, the Scottish sculptor who created a famous garden at Stonypath, Lanarkshire. Christensen (b. 1949) places him in the very different, exotic Cactus Garden at the Huntington Library in Pasadena.

"

... the public must learn how to cherish the nobler and rarer plants

"

MARGARET FULLER (1810–50)

Salvatore **PULVIRENTI**
Untitled
1995

This landscape is conjured up from the very simplest of elements—a pot plant, a smooth pebble, a piece of board on a table, plus some oddly shaped rocks nearby. The arrangement on the table splits the kind of view people admire into its minimalist component parts and offers these up for contemplation.

قبر النبي صلى الله عليه
قبر ابو بكر

"*The day in his hotness;*
The strife with the palm;
The night in her silence,
The stars in her calm."

MATTHEW ARNOLD (1822–88)

View of Medina and the Mosque of the Prophet Mohammed, Ottoman Turkish
date unknown

This sparse desert view, with the town and mosque surrounded by barren hills and a few clumps of palms, helps to explain Islamic culture's traditional fascination with running water and gardens.

“

O Love what hours were thine and mine,
In lands of palm and southern pine;
In lands of palm, of orange-blossom,
Of olive, aloe, and maize and vine.

”

ALFRED, LORD TENNYSON (1809–92)

Tofat **AL-AHRAR**
Two Princesses in a Garden, Bokhara
1568

This exquisite miniature makes an implied comparison between the beauty of the two young women and that of the stylized garden they stand in. Bokhara is in Uzbekistan, and in the late sixteenth century it achieved its greatest political and cultural importance.

Sir Lawrence **ALMA-TADEMA**
Unconscious Rivals
1893

Sir Lawrence Alma-Tadema (1836–1912) here attempted to travel in time and space. The terrace, with its oleander flowering in a metal tub, overlooks the sea—the Mediterranean of the artist's imagination. The two women are meant to be ancient Romans.

Bread Fruit

attributed to
Sydney **PARKINSON**
Bread Fruit
c. 1769

This fine botanical drawing was made on board the *Bounty*, around twenty years before the famous mutiny. The ship was transporting breadfruit trees from Tahiti to the West Indies. The picture is a reminder of the way in which the flora of different regions of the world became intermingled, thanks to the pressing urge for exploration and colonization.

Carlos **FORNS BADA**
Prickly Pears
1996

Prickly pears are the fruit of a species of cactus that originates in the western hemisphere. These plants have now spread to Australia and southern Africa. The most widely cultivated kind, the Indian fig, is grown chiefly in Mexico. Forns Bada (b. 1963) here seems to equate their spines with those in Christ's crown of thorns.

Albert **BIERSTADT**
California Redwoods
1860s

One of the most spectacular of all species of tree, California redwoods can grow to over 300 feet tall. They can also live to be 4,000 years old and were once reputed to be the oldest living things—a title that they have now lost to their close relative, the bristle-cone pine.

Carlo **BERTOCCI**
Giotto
1998–99

Bertocci (b. 1946) probably named this picture as a tribute to the painter Giotto (1266/76–1342). The four youths in the foreground are, the picture implies, at the beginning of a journey. The potted bay tree sharing the ledge with them suggests that it is a journey toward artistic fame.

Georges **CLAIRIN**
The Peacock Garden
Early 20th century

An elaborate *fin-de-siècle* fantasy of harem life, this is related to the decors the Russian painter Leon Bakst (1866–1924) produced for Serge Diaghilev's Ballet Russe, notably for its spectacular production of *Schéhérazade* (1910). This revived the fashion for Orientalism, popular almost throughout the nineteenth century, and disseminated it all over Europe.

John Frederick **LEWIS**
In the Bey's Garden
1865

Like his contemporary Edward Lear (1812–88), John Frederick Lewis (1805–76) traveled widely in the Middle East, recording what he saw in exceptionally meticulous style. This painting, however, shows something the artist can never have seen with his own eyes—the wife or concubine of a high Turkish official, unveiled and arranging flowers in her private garden.

following page ▶
Admiral Sir Edward Augustus **INGLEFIELD**
The Blue Mountains, Jamaica
1879

Inglefield (1820–94) was one of the numerous British officers, military as well as naval, who were highly skilled amateur artists. The Victorian public often got its first glimpses of the huge scenic variety of the British Empire thanks to their efforts. This view of the Blue Mountains in Jamaica is a faithful rendition of the lush vegetation found there. The remote areas of the island look much the same today, though women traveling to market (such as the sole figure shown) no longer wear such traditional dress.

> "*For the life in them he loved*
> *most living things,*
> *But a tree chiefly.*"

PHILIP EDWARD THOMAS (1878–1917)

Ando **HIROSHIGE**
Maples at Mama
1857

Series of views of famous beauty spots became popular in Japan in the mid-nineteenth century and were produced in quantity by both Hiroshige (1797–1858) and his contemporary and rival Katushika Hokusai (1760–1849). This painting comes from a set of prints called "100 Views of Famous Places in Edo." (Edo is the old name for Tokyo.) The maple trees shown would have been cultivated chiefly for their ornamental qualities.

Dorothy
HENRIQUES WELLS
Poinciana
1990s

The poinciana tree originated in Madagascar but has become widely disseminated in tropical and subtropical regions elsewhere. In particular it flourishes in the West Indies and the Bahamas. This beautiful specimen was painted by a contemporary Jamaican artist. The watercolor shows the Blue Mountains in the background.

dorothy henriques Wells

Albert **BIERSTADT**
The Majesty of the Mountains
1860s

Bierstadt (1830–1902) traveled to parts of America that were then unsettled. These journeys resulted in numerous paintings that gave his contemporaries a new and romantic idea of the scenic wonders of the North American continent. These places were, at the time, known to comparatively few people.

William **DANIELL**
South-east view of the Hill Fort of Bijaigaih, Bihar
1830s

This work shows the artist himself sketching in the shade of an awning held by two Indian attendants. His elder brother and fellow artist Thomas (1749–1840), who accompanied him on all his travels, is taking a pot-shot at a passing bird.

Kendhal Jan **JUBB**
Four Lemons
1998

The artist has placed an unusual mixture of plants together in this painting. Exotic bromeliads and halyconia from Hawaii are combined with lemons, which are a familiar European staple.

Henri **ROUSSEAU**
Virgin Forest at Sunset, with a Negro Attacked by a Leopard
1907

Rousseau's (1844–1910) jungle scenes were almost entirely the products of his imagination. They seem to have been inspired by visits to the hothouses at the Exposition Universelle held in Paris in 1889, and the Jardin des Plantes. However, Rousseau himself claimed to have fought in Mexico as one of the soldiers of the Emperor Maximilian. Rousseau's fantasies show the hold that the exotic worlds discovered by eighteenth- and nineteenth-century explorers had over the minds of those back at home.

Henri Rousseau

José Maria **VELASCO**
A Small Volcano in Mexico
1887

The pictorial conventions Velasco (1840–1912) uses derive from European landscape painting of the seventeenth and eighteenth centuries, but the landscapes he portrays are unmistakably exotic. Here, the volcano vividly suggests the latent violence of the Mexican landscape.

Hank **PITCHER**
Pyramid Peak
1998

Pyramid Peak is situated within the vicinity of Santa Barbara, and is composed of multiple points that Pitcher has rendered to look like ancient pyramids. The tropical flowers along the coastline enhance this stunning view.

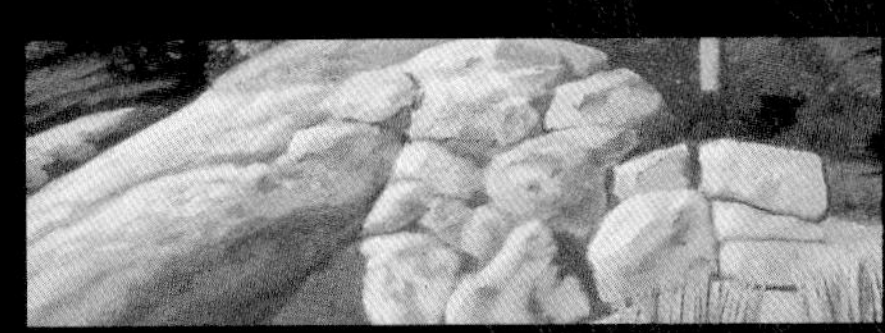

CHAPTER SEVEN

arcadian landscape

"...it must display the natural beauties, and hide the natural defects of every situation..."

HUMPHREY REPTON (1752–1818)

David **LIGARE**
Landscape with Diana and Acteon (detail)
1996

IF ONE OF THE LITERARY SOURCES for the ideal of the perfect garden was the Bible, another, certainly from the late seventeenth century onward, was classical literature, and, more specifically, the *Idylls* of the Hellenistic pastoral poet Theocritus (c. 300–260BC). These idylls feature shepherds, shepherdesses, and wood nymphs, and they have had a long-lasting, deep impact upon European literature. For example, Virgil's *Eclogues* (42–37BC) were modeled directly on them—so, too, was Milton's *Lycidas* (1638).

David **LIGARE**
Landscape with Diana and Acteon
(detail)
1996

The setting for Theocritus's poems is Sicily, but this was territory not much frequented by seventeenth-century artists. The city that drew them was Rome, and surrounding Rome was the Campagna, a lowland plain which, since the catastrophes of the early Middle Ages, had had a surprisingly deserted aspect for an area so close

Sir Edward
BURNE-JONES
The Garden Court, from the "Briar Rose" series
(detail)
1890

to a great city. It became notorious for lawlessness and banditry and provided the inspiration for the paintings of bandits in which Salvator Rosa (1615–73) metaphorically celebrated the wildness and freedom of his own vocation as a painter. Foreign artists coming to live and work in Rome took a kinder view of it. The most influential of these foreigners was the Frenchman Claude Lorraine (1600–82), Rosa's exact contemporary.

Claude was not a man of much education—according to his original biographer, Joachim von Sandrart, he was first apprenticed to a pastry cook—but he took the Theocritan tradition that had for so long flourished in literature and gave it a seductive, visible form. His ideal landscapes, based on sketching trips made to the Campagna, created a vision of a landscape haunted by antiquity.

Eugene Samuel
GRASSET
Young Lady in a Garden
(detail)
Early 20th century

F ONE OF THE LITERARY SOURCES for the ideal of the perfect garden was the Bible, another, certainly from the late seventeenth century onwards, was classical literature, and, more specifically, the *Idylls* of the Hellenistic pastoral poet Theocritus (c. 300–260BC). These idylls feature shepherds, shepherdesses and wood nymphs, and they have had a long-lasting, deep impact upon European literature. For example, Virgil's *Eclogues* (42–37BC) were modelled directly on them – so, too, was Milton's *Lycidas* (1638).

Henryk **SIEMIRADZKI**
Rest
1896

Pierre **PUVIS DE CHAVANNES**
Between Art and Nature
(detail)
1890

The setting for Theocritus's poems is Sicily, but this was territory not much frequented by seventeenth-century artists. The city that drew them was Rome, and surrounding Rome was the Campagna, a lowland plain which, since the catastrophes of the early Middle Ages, had had a surprisingly preferred artist of his mistress, Mme de Pompadour—created light-hearted pastoral scenes side by side with frivolous retellings of classical mythology. Small figures of shepherds and shepherdesses were produced in quantity by the great porcelain factories of the time—Meissen, Nymphenburg, and Sèvres. They also produced great numbers of porcelain flowers and tableware in which flowers, both molded and painted, played a prominent part in the decoration. Porcelain was also used to make tureens and other vessels that imitated vegetables—a tradition that descended from the sixteenth-century French potter Bernard Palissy (1509–90), though Palissy was usually keener on snakes and other creepy-crawlies than he was on garden vegetables.

Sir Lawrence **ALMA-TADEMA** *Flora—Spring in the Gardens of the Villa Borghese* 1880s

Rococo pastoral is a curious hybrid. It pays tribute to the idea of the "natural" while confining everything to a realm of artificiality.

“*But she lost all consciousness of herself by-and-by when the party strolled out into the beautiful gardens.*”

ELIZABETH GASKELL (1810–65)

Sir Lawrence
ALMA-TADEMA
Flora – Spring in the Gardens of the Villa Borghese
1880s

Alma-Tadema (1836–1912) here offers a scene from contemporary life; something very unusual for an artist who was usually concerned with Roman antiquity. The young woman he depicts appears to be English, as she wears a version of the English Aesthetic Movement dress.

Henryk **SIEMIRADZKI**
Rest
1896

By a Polish artist, this painting nevertheless seems to show an idealized scene somewhere in the foothills of the Italian Alps. Throughout the nineteenth century Italy swarmed with non-Italian artists, drawn there by the beauty of the scenery and the inhabitants, as well as by the presence of so many masterpieces from the past.

Eugene Samuel
GRASSET
Young Lady in a Garden
Early 20th century

The work of a Swiss artist strongly under the influence of the British Pre-Raphaelites, this painting conjures up a dream world that combines Neoclassical, Biedermeier, and medieval elements. The eclectic artistic climate of this time supplied the context for the Modernist revolt led by the Fauves in 1905.

Auguste **RAYNAUD**
Watering the Garden
Late 19th century

Nineteenth-century academic art seized upon almost any excuse it could find for erotic display. Here, the nudity of the young gardener, who is presumably meant to be a slave girl in an ancient Roman household, powerfully reinforces the sexual symbolism of the action that is being portrayed.

◀ *previous page*
Tito **MARCI**
Parting 1
1998

This shows the traditional Arcadian landscape stripped to the bare bones – a tree, a flat coastline, a pile of rocks and some distant hills. Though there are twin figures in the work, each seems isolated. The picture can be read as an allegory of the contemporary concept of the 'divided self'.

"And eke attonce the heavy trees they climb, Which seem to labour under their fruits' load."

EDMUND SPENSER (c.1552–99)

Robin **PALANKER**
Villa I
1991

This is a good example of the way in which classical garden design, with its reliance on architectural elements, continues to influence contemporary painters.

Jan **VAN KESSEL THE ELDER**
Vertumnus and Pomona
Mid-17th century

The story of Vertumnus and Pomona comes from Ovid's *Metamorphoses, Book 14*. In it, Vertumnus, protector of gardens, woos Pomona, goddess of ripening fruit, in various rustic disguises, finally appearing to her as he is seen here – disguised as an old woman. Van Kessel (1626–79) has used the story as an excuse to create a virtuoso display of flowers and fruit.

"The maiden pleasance of the land
Knoweth no stir of voice or hand.
No cup the sleeping waters fill,
The restless shuttle lieth still."

WILLIAM MORRIS (1834–96)

Sir Edward **BURNE-JONES**
The Garden Court, from the "Briar Rose" series
1890

The "Briar Rose" series retells the story of the Sleeping Beauty. Here the princess's attendants slumber in the loggia of her palace, hemmed in by almost impenetrable thickets of climbing roses that cut them off from the everyday world.

Ubaldo **BARTOLINI**
The Washerwoman's Return
1997

The contemporary Italian painter Bartolini (b. 1944) creates imaginary "capriccio" landscapes in the style of predecessors such as Paul Brill (1554–1626), a Flemish artist who spent his career in Italy. In this painting the invented landscape is given added meaning by the presence of a solitary figure.

Jean-Baptiste
Camille **COROT**
View of Florence from the Boboli Gardens
1834

Corot's (1796–1875) panorama of Florence, with the Duomo and the Palazzo Vecchio both clearly visible, combines realism and idealism. The view is topographically accurate, but the golden light that bathes the landscape speaks mainly about the rapture the artist felt when contemplating this famous view.

Salvo **RUSSO**
Triad
1991

The "Triad" of the title is the group of three fanciful constructions that forms the main subject of the painting. The painting is influenced by the Tuscan landscapes that appear in the backgrounds of the religious works by Renaissance artists such as Fra Bartolommeo (1472–1517).

> "*So twice five miles of fertile ground*
> *With walls and towers were girdled round.*"
>
> **SAMUEL TAYLOR COLERIDGE**
>
> (1772–1834)

Salvatore **PULVIRENTI**
Toward the Time
1998

This composition offers a painting within a painting, which in turn contrasts flowering new growth with fragments of romantic ruin. The implication is that the perfect moment hovers forever out of reach.

◀ *previous page*
Pierre **PUVIS DE CHAVANNES**
Between Art and Nature
1890

This painting is unusual for the artist because it shows some of the figures in contemporary dress, rather than in a version of classical costume. The general atmosphere of Arcadian tranquility is, however, typical of Puvis' work. The industrial late nineteenth century found such compositions deeply soothing.

Figure of a shepherdess, Bow porcelain
c. 1765
Figures of this kind celebrate the cult of rustic innocence and prettiness that was so prevalent in the mid-eighteenth century. Such pieces were originally used as part of elaborate table decorations, and they replaced similar figures made of sugar.

“*Pleasures newly found are sweet*
When they lie about our feet...”

WILLIAM WORDSWORTH (1770–1850)

Jacques de **LAJOUE**
Oriental Garden
Early 18th century

Lajoue here takes ideas directly from Watteau's *fêtes champêtres* and places them into an Oriental context. The basic setting—a park with statues—is very similar to those favored by Watteau (*see page 38*), but here the fountain is crowned with Islamic crescents, and the male figures are clothed in Oriental dress.

“

Spring, the sweet spring,
is the year's pleasant king;
Then blooms each thing,
then maids dance in a ring...

”

THOMAS NASHE (1567–1601)

Thomas Matthews **ROOKE**
The Dancing Girls
c. 1882

This is a mock-Renaissance rendering of an outdoor celebration at a Tuscan villa. The atmosphere of the work, however, remains decorously late Victorian.

Claude-Joseph **VERNET**
The Villa Pamphili
1749

The great Italian gardens created by earlier generations of architects and gardeners in Italy fascinated French eighteenth-century artists who visited the Italian peninsula. This is a soberly factual rendering of one of the great Italian villa gardens on the outskirts of Rome.

"*I think there are as many different kinds of gardening as poetry.*"

JOSEPH ADDISON (1672–1719)

Silvano **D'AMBROSIO**
Wandering Perfumes
1999

The title suggests that the flowering tree in the center of the composition pervades the entire landscape, surrounding it with the sweetness of its scent and therefore adding a deeply emotional tone to the whole panorama.

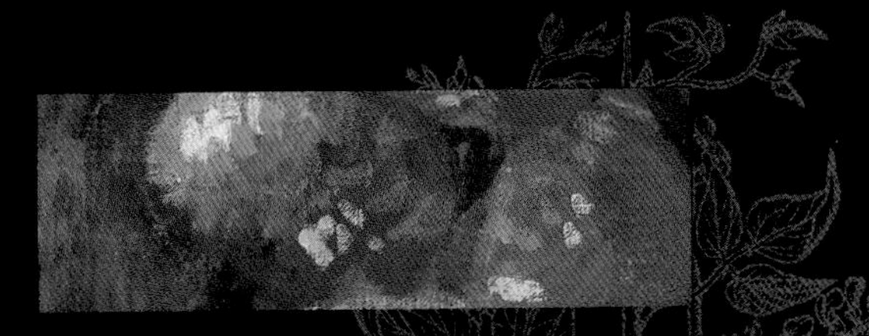

CHAPTER EIGHT

the bounty of nature

"What wond'rous life is this I lead!
Ripe apples drop about my head;
The luscious clusters of the vine
Upon my mouth do crush their wine"

ANDREW MARVELL (1621–78)

Paul **SERUSIER**
Still Life with Onions
c. 1896

IMITATIONS OF FLOWERS and fruits in porcelain and other ceramic materials are only a small part of the interface between nature and art. However, what is delightful about a porcelain simulacrum of a blossom or even of some humble vegetable—the lifelike cauliflower, for example, which turns out to be a receptacle for cauliflower soup—is not just the accuracy with which the particular object is replicated, but the implied contrast between the ephemeral and the quasi-eternal. Imitations of objects from the vegetable kingdom are more successful in stating this paradox than models of animals, or, indeed, than likenesses of human beings. The reason is that there is less room for the subjective, for the intervention of the concept of style. A porcelain fruit, for example, can be directly molded from the original.

Michael
LEONARD
Cabbages, Onions, and Radishes
(detail)
1994

Paul **GAUGUIN**
Still Life for the Fête at Gloanec
(detail)
1888

The approach to painting flowers and fruit is different. The still life as an independent genre made a tentative appearance in Greek and Roman art, but then disappeared from view until the end of the fifteenth or the beginning of the sixteenth century. Its reappearance was heralded by the decorations featuring naturalistically painted flowers, which fill a number of fifteenth-century manuscripts, most of them emanating from workshops in the Flemish city of Bruges. While the earliest independent still life is Italian, painted by Jacopo de'Barbari in 1504, the still-life genre became a specialty of northern artists. Many of the earliest still lifes have an allegorical purpose, featuring items such as skulls, candles, and hourglasses as emblems of human mortality. Others combine

Michael **WENTZEL**
Fruit and Flower Still Life
(detail)
1829

flowers and fruits from different seasons, their aim being to cram the whole cycle of the seasons into a single canvas. Painters kept notebooks in which to record the appearance of different flowers at different times of the year. They were then able to combine them into bouquets that could never have existed in reality.

Carlo
BERTOCCI
Piety on High
1996

Only gradually did still-life painting move toward the faithful replication of what the painter actually saw in front of him. As it did so, what can be described as a specialty within a specialty developed: the production of *trompe l'oeil* paintings that were designed to deceive the spectator into believing that what he or she saw was not a simulacrum, but reality itself. In general, however, painters preferred to create these using manufactured rather than natural objects, though

Henri
ROUSSEAU
Bunch of Flowers
c. 1909–10

wreaths of flowers were occasionally used as subjects for this kind of work. The reason for choosing wreaths was because successful *trompe l'oeil* depends on the objects concerned being presented against a background that is very close to the picture-plane itself—a wreath hung on a wall is of course ideal for this purpose.

Artists also used the forms of flowers, fruit, and vegetables to shape likenesses of human beings and animals. The most famous examples of these are the work of the Milanese painter Giuseppe Arcimboldo (c. 1527–93), who spent a large part of his career working for the Hapsburg Emperor Rudolph II in Prague. The components chosen to make up one of his "portraits" would usually be related to some emblematic or allegorical programme; a figure of Winter might show the likeness of an old man and be made up of different root vegetables.

Jose **FILLOL**
The Orange Harvest
(detail)
Late 19th/Early 20th century

Paula
MODERSOHN-BECKER
Still Life with a Yellow Bowl
1906

This deliberately quiet and humble still life reflects the impact made on Modersohn-Becker (1876–1907) by the work of the French Post-Impressionists, particularly Gauguin (1848–1903). Probably painted in her hotel room in Paris after she had separated from her husband to return there alone, it achieves a rich sunny effect through very simple means.

Michael **WENTZEL**
Fruit and Flower Still Life
1829

Dutch seventeenth-century paintings often contain small allusions to human mortality—a fly or a caterpillar for example, which also portrays the artist's satisfaction with the here and now, the life of the senses. Notable here is the inclusion of a pineapple, still very much an exotic fruit during the epoch this work was painted.

"

Who of men, can tell
That flowers would bloom,
Or that green fruit
would Swell

"

JOHN KEATS (1795–1821)

Carlo **BERTOCCI**
Piety on High
1996

At first sight a simple genre scene; at a second glance slightly surrealist. Kneeling on a chair raised on flowerpots the child prays, not to the image of a saint, but to a fruiting lemon tree —nature incarnate.

Jacquelyn **MCBAIN**
New Haloes
1994

This simple still life, in the Dutch tradition, focuses on the hues of unpeeled and partly peeled oranges. At the center of the canvas the flesh of the partly peeled fruit catches the light with a jewel-like blaze.

Fête Gloanec
Madeleine

Paul **GAUGUIN**
Still Life for the Fête at Gloanec
1888

Gauguin (1848–1903) often went hungry in his Breton period. Having once been a prosperous stockbroker, he had given up a great deal for his art. This radiant still life, with pears and loaves of bread, conveys the excitement of a special day, when unusually luxurious types of food were available.

Alfredo **RAMOS MARTINEZ**
Flower Sellers
1930s

Ramos Martinez (1872–1946) portrays, in a stylish Deco painting, the itinerant Mexican Indian flower-sellers who also fascinated his contemporary Diego Rivera (1886–1957).

"*I, with as easy hunger take*
entire my season's dole—
welcome the ripe, the sweet, the sour,
the hollow and the whole."

LAURIE LEE (1914–97)

Paul **GAUGUIN**
Still Life with Mangoes (detail)
c. 1896

Gauguin (1848–1903) here suggests the richness of tropical nature through a casual arrangement of fruit. These fruits would themselves be things that very few members of his intended audience back home in France had tasted, since this was still in the days before refrigeration. He was thus flaunting the adventurous nature of his own career and his willingness to seek new sensations.

“

Where'er you tread,
the blushing flowers shall rise,
And all things flourish
where you turn your eyes.

”

ALEXANDER POPE (1688–1744)

Odilon **REDON**
Flowers in a Turquoise Vase
1905

Having made an initial reputation as a powerful printmaker, Redon (1840–1916) began to produce flower studies in pastel in the mid-1880s. His flowers burn with an inner fire that makes them seem like emanations of the life-force itself.

Henri **MATISSE**
Still Life with Flowers and a Plate of Fruit
1947

This black and white drawing offers a good example of Matisse's (1869–1954) power to suggest colour even when it is absent. The simplified forms he uses here seem full of life – we can easily imagine the brilliant hues of the objects he has drawn.

H. Matisse 47

John Singer **SARGENT**
Thou Shalt Not Steal
1918

At the end of his career Sargent (1856–1925) spent a period as an official war artist. What attracted his eye at this time were small incidents like the one represented here, in a watercolor showing soldiers taking ripe fruit from an orchard near Arras. There is a poignant contrast between nature's bounty and the harsh reality of war.

Carl **LARSSON**
The Apple Harvest
Early 20th century

The slightly sentimental paintings and illustrations of the Swedish artist Carl Larsson (1853–1919) created a fashion for the studied, subtly rustic, simplicity that lingers to this day. He is the undoubted progenitor of today's "Swedish style" in interior decoration.

Paul **GAUGUIN**
Rupe Rupe (Gathering Fruit)
1899

This painting was done in Tahiti, at a time when Gauguin (1848–1903) was entering into his final phase as an artist. This frieze like composition has an air of melancholy, but is nevertheless also a celebration of nature's abundance. Like many other artists, Gauguin here compares the natural ripeness of the female form with the general abundance of nature.

Wes **CHRISTENSEN**
D'où venons-nous?
1990

The contemporary American artist Wes Christensen (b. 1949) has borrowed part of the title of Gauguin's most important Tahiti-period painting, *Where do we come from? Where are we going?* His female figure contemplates emblems of death and life: on the one hand an ancient Egyptian canopic jar, made to hold the viscera of a corpse; and on the other a luscious bowl of peaches.

Jose **FILLOL**

The Orange Harvest

Late 19th/Early 20th century

This represents a slightly cleaned up and sweetened idea of life in rural Spain – a country that was to plunge into a savage civil war not so very long after the picture was painted. Notable is the opposition that it proposes between men and women; the girls all on one side of the composition, the men on the other.

ANONYMOUS

Autumn

Early 19th century

Making paintings on the reverse side of a piece of glass, otherwise called *verre eglomisé*, was a traditional Bavarian peasant craft. These slightly naïve works were particularly admired by the artists of the avant-garde Blaue Reiter group in the early years of the twentieth century.

Lucas Van **VALKENBORCH**
Spring
1595

This painting tries to combine portraiture, genre, and allegory. The lady to the right, despite her apron, is richly dressed, though the black and white of her costume suggests she may be a widow. The young girl to her left is even more luxuriously clothed. The painting therefore suggests hope for a new generation, and is perhaps celebrating an impending marriage.

Stefano di **STASIO**
Woman
1988

For Stefano di Stasio (b. 1948) natural fecundity is literally female—he portrays nature allegorically, as a female nude masked with flowers, with a full moon shining above her.

Michael **LEONARD**
Strawberries
1993

Leonard's (b. 1933) extreme skill in rendering color and tone is here applied to the very simplest of still-life subjects. The result prompts comparison with two great predecessors, the Dutchman Adriaen Coorte (working 1683–1723) and the Frenchman Jean-Baptiste Chardin (1699–1779).

"*Wife unto the garden*
and set me a plot
With strawberry roots
of the best to be got"

THOMAS TUSSER (1524–80)

Carlos **FORNS BADA**
Crowned Gardner
1996

The young gardener, his clothes patterned with strawberries, is here shown as the king of nature. The strawberries of Michael Leonard's painting (opposite) have migrated to become ornaments on his clothing. Artists of the seventeenth or eighteenth century would have used this idea to create a costume for a figure in a masque.

Robert **FURBER**
December
1732

A hand-colored engraving from a *Catalog of Fruits* arranged according to season. Each fruit variety—apples, grapes, and pears—is listed in the text below the plate, as are other inedible fruits like the berries of arbutus and holly.

Robert **BISSELL**
The Wages of Sin
1996

The artist has here taken a hint from the still-life painting of the past, which often turns an assemblage of objects into a symbolic *memento mori*. Here, however, the concept is drastically simplified—two wasps have started to attack an apple that has had a bite taken out of it.

"Let my beloved come into his garden, and eat his pleasant fruits."

SONG OF SONGS 2:16

Georg **FLEGEL**
Man and Woman Before a Table
Early 17th century

This painting, in general, is about the idea of abundance. The piled up fruits and vegetables symbolize this though, like the flowers in the vase (*see page 252*), they are all available at different times of the year. There is also, however, a more directly sexual connotation—the man embraces the woman as she touches a basket of peaches, which, because of their form, are often a sexual symbol. The implication, therefore, is that she is either already pregnant, or will soon become so.

John **NAVA**
Casablanca Lilies
1999

This simple vase of lilies glows with light that is the equivalent of the "glamor lighting" invented by Hollywood stills photographers in the 1930s. It makes the flowers seem more real than reality itself.

Roman mosaic
Basket of Flowers
1st century AD

This decorative basket of flowers seems much more modern than it is because of its similarity to the work of painters of the seventeenth and eighteenth centuries. The objective of this work is the same as theirs was—to offer an image of natural abundance. Only the actual technique is different.

> “*Here are fruits, flowers,*
> *leaves and branches*
> *And here also is my heart*
> *which beats only for you.*”

Paul Verlaine (1844–96)

Henri **ROUSSEAU**
Bunch of Flowers
c. 1909–10

Rousseau's (1844–1910) flowers are not lifelike, any more than his jungle scenes are. Nevertheless he does manage to convey a sense of the energy within nature. These flowers may not have much to do with reality as most people see it, but they have great presence, due chiefly to the artist's feeling for rhythmic pattern.

Giuseppe
ARCIMBOLDO
Flora
1591

The late Mannerist painter Giuseppe Arcimboldo (1527–93) is now chiefly remembered for his extraordinary proto-surrealist heads. Each head is composed of flowers or fruit or even kitchen implements. Many seem to have been intended as caricatures, ridiculing their subjects. Here, the artist, in a much gentler vein, symbolizes spring with the head of a court lady entirely composed of flowers and flower petals.

Martha Mayer
ERLEBACHER
Close Encounter
1984

Best known for her paintings of classical figures, Martha Erlebacher (b. 1937) here offers an amusing updating of Arcimboldo, in a head made of various kinds of vegetables. The chief component is a green pepper, which takes a grotesque anthropomorphic shape. The title alludes to Steven Spielberg's (b. 1947) science fiction film, *Close Encounters of the Third Kind*.

> *Let me be dress'd fine as I will,*
> *Flies, worms, and flowers, exceed me still.*

ISAAC WATTS (1674–1748)

Mogul artist
Flowers
1633–42

In addition to illustrating texts, Mogul artists painted independent compositions, which were then assembled into albums. This drawing comes from an album made for Dara Shikoh, who, at the time, was the expected successor to his father, Emperor Shah Jahan (1628–58). He was in fact executed by his brother.

William **MORRIS**
The Strawberry Thief
1883

The most famous of all William Morris's (1834–96) textile designs, this demonstrates his extraordinary talent for creating complex patterns from simple elements borrowed from the natural world.

Anthony **HOLDSWORTH**
Zucchini
(detail)
1995

Farmers' markets have become increasingly popular in the United States. Consumers like the direct contact with the growers, and feel that the produce they buy is likely to be fresher than that found in supermarkets. This skillfully executed realist painting therefore represents an increasingly familiar scene, which in turn seems to reflect the genuine changes in American society.

Michael **LEONARD**

Cabbages, Onions, and Radishes

1994

Michael Leonard (b. 1933) is chiefly interested in creating abstract patterns of solid and void within the rectangle of the picture frame. The warmth of color comes from the purple blush on some of the cabbage leaves, which is carefully tuned to the red and bronze hues of the radishes and large onions. As an example of making much out of little it can be compared to the Modersohn-Becker (1876–1907) image on page 244.

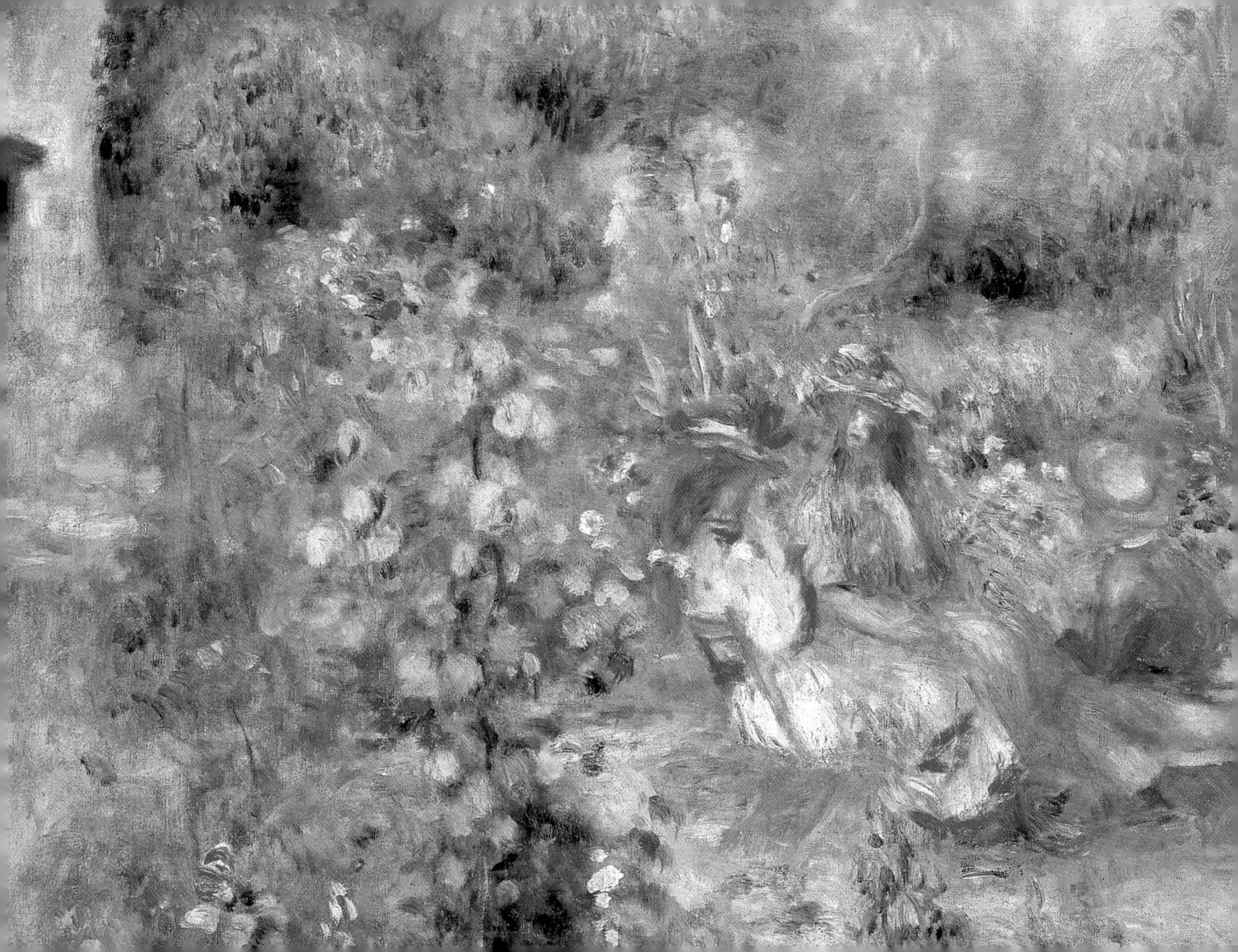

CHAPTER NINE

my own little plot

"We must cultivate our own garden."

VOLTAIRE (FRANÇOIS MARIE AROUET) (1694–1778)

Pierre-Auguste **RENOIR**
Young Girls in the Garden at Montmartre
1893–95

THE ACTIVITIES of the great eighteenth- and nineteenth-century plant collectors had the effect of enormously widening the choice of plants that European and North American gardeners had available to them. In one sense this had a destructive effect on standards of garden design. Many nineteenth-century gardens became strange mixtures of plants of different types, brought together with little thought for their overall effect. But there were also positive results. Thanks both to new imports and selective propagation, flowering seasons became much longer. Whereas the medieval garden had been in full bloom for only a few short weeks, gardens of the late nineteenth and early twentieth centuries could be persuaded to flower almost all year round.

Annabel
GOSLING
The Red Bucket
(detail)
1997

During this time, there was also a democratization of gardening. The ideal cottage garden, seductively represented

Vincent
VAN GOGH
Mlle. Gachet in Her Garden
1890

in many immensely skillful Victorian watercolors, was first created during a period when the rural poor enjoyed at least a little more leisure time than had been available to them before. The small gardens they cultivated for themselves were assertions of a new independence. These gardens often made more use of annual and biennial plants than they did of more ambitious types of cultivation, as the aim was to pack as much color and variety as possible into a very small space.

Theo **VAN RYSSELBERGHE**
Garden Flowers
date unknown

The rise of the cottage garden led, in turn, to a kind of idealization of the esthetic and social values it seemed to represent. The leader of this movement was Gertrude Jekyll (1843–1942), the garden designer who worked in close collaboration with the architect Sir Edwin Lutyens (1869–1944). Lutyens' early country houses, built before

World War I, were in a vernacular style and cultivated qualities of "simplicity and directness," which he claimed to have learned from Jekyll. She, in turn, drew part of her inspiration from the teachings of John Ruskin (1819–1900), who believed that the close study of natural forms should be the main source of inspiration for the fine artist. Jekyll's elaboration on this was to find, in the orderly disorder of the supposedly artless and unsophisticated cottage garden, an inspiration for much more ambitious design structures.

Ian **GARDNER**
Red Cabbage
(detail)
1996

Camille
PISSARRO
Woman at Work in a Garden
c. 1890

At about the same period that Jekyll's influence became dominant in garden design, people began to take an interest in the history of gardens—not merely in the different ways of planning and constructing gardens, but in old garden tools and old methods of cultivation.

In Britain, the continuing movement of people from the country into towns—something that had started in the mid-eighteenth century with the first stirrings of the Industrial Revolution—gave rise to a phenomenon that was related to the cottage garden, the allotment. The word, used in relation to land, has a wide variety of different meanings, each associated with a particular culture or society. The *Concise Oxford Dictionary*, choosing the British usage, defines it as "a small piece of land rented (usually from a local authority) for cultivation." Allotments are cottage gardens without their attendant cottages, where dwellers in towns can cultivate the soil. The emphasis is not on flowers but on vegetables, and there is often keen competition to see who can grow the largest vegetable. The competitive camaraderie of a group of neighboring allotments creates a small society that is complete in itself.

Pierre-Auguste **RENOIR** *Woman with Parasol in the Garden* (detail) 1873

Annabel **GOSLING**
The Red Bucket
1997

Still somewhat in the Impressionist tradition, this vigorous, broadly painted study once again, like the picture opposite, closes off the spectator's view, offering the merest glimpse of a private domain. In this case, the domain in question seems to be a Mediterranean one. The plants are very generalized, but they all seem to be tough-leafed species, resistant to heat and lack of moisture.

Alfred Jean **CHAGNIOT**
Lady Painting in Her Garden
1930s

This belated Impressionist here tackles a subject often seen in true Impressionist art—a painter working *en plein air*. Among the things one notes here are the immaculate costume and the restricted scale. The lady lays claim to her domain by portraying, on a canvas of very modest size, a bouquet of garden flowers placed in a rustic jug on a metal table. Everything is carefully scaled down—not too ambitious.

Kate **GREENAWAY**

Mary, Mary, Quite Contrary

1900

This color lithograph comes from one of the immensely successful children's books that Greenaway (1846–1901) illustrated. In this case the illustration is for the traditional rhyme "Mary, Mary, quite contrary/ How does your garden grow?..." Greenaway's work is in a sweeter and more simpering version of the Carl Larsson style (*see page 255*). One notable aspect is her attachment to anachronistic neo-Regency costume. This was the beginning of a fashion for the greater "simplicity" of the early nineteenth century that was to be fostered a little later, and more surprisingly, by some of Diaghilev's (1872–1929) early ballets.

"

O the green things growing... The faint sweet smell of the green things growing!

"

DINAH MULOCK CRAIK (1826–87)

Angela **VOLPI**

The Country Round

1998

The balloons dangling from the trees suggest that this is the moment for some traditional country festival. The young man's working clothes, on the other hand, suggest that not too much time can be devoted to it.

But Peter, who was very naughty, ran straight away to Mr MacGregor's garden and squeezed under the gate.

"

BEATRIX POTTER (1866–1943)

Wes **CHRISTENSEN**
Looking for Peter
1992

Who is Peter? The artist has actually created an intricate and intimate domain for Potter's Peter Rabbit. But where is he? In the mysterious shed? Or simply concealed behind one of the thick hedges?

Ian **GARDNER**
Red Cabbage
1996

The contemporary English painter Ian Gardner (b. 1944), once an adherent of the avant-garde, has become an enthusiast for the late eighteenth-century watercolor wash-on-wash technique, of which this is an example. He also enjoys working on one of the allotments on the outskirts of the small town of Lancaster, where he now lives. The composition stresses the extreme neatness with which good allotments are kept.

“

And the LORD God planted a garden eastwards in Eden; and there he put the man whom he had formed.

”

GENESIS 2:8–9

Ian **GARDNER**
Diane
1996

Another, more open view of Gardner's allotment. The fluttering red pennants, used to subtle compositional effect, are to scare away birds, and the female figure in the background, near the small greenhouse, is the artist's wife, Diane. Most of what the allotment produces is destined for her kitchen.

◀ *previous page*
Maud **NAFTEL**
Tending the Cabbage Patch
(detail)
c. 1880

A variant of the "cottage garden" style that is also represented here by several other paintings. These are not exactly the rural poor—the house is too large for that—but the implication is that its occupiers have fallen on hard times. To a large extent, it is this that makes them and their surroundings suitably picturesque.

Theo **VAN RYSSELBERGHE**
Garden Flowers
date unknown

Van Rysselberghe (1862–1926) contrives a play between "inside" and "outside." The girl is in a garden room—an adjunct of many prosperous middle-class homes. She is arranging flowers that were presumably gathered in the garden. The picked flowers crowd against the large windows.

"

I have a garden of my own,
But so with roses overgrown,
And lilies, that you would it guess
To be a little wilderness.

"

ANDREW MARVELL (1621–78)

Erasmus **RITTER VON ENGERT**
Garden of a Viennese House
1829–30

This depiction of an early nineteenth-century Viennese town garden is almost comically prim, though the tall sunflower and the hollyhocks both seem inclined to rebel against the narrow space in which they are confined. The tone is, however, set by the presiding figure—a young woman seated in an upright chair, who is simultaneously knitting and reading the Bible perched on her lap.

John George **SOWERBY**
The Box Seats
Early 20th century

A typical English "cottage garden" painting of the early years of the twentieth century, of a kind produced by scores of talented artists. The special features here are the two box plants, clipped into the form of thrones. The fact that they are quite suitable to sit on adds to their eccentric, slightly surrealist attraction.

Ernest **WALBOURN**
The Garden Path
c. 1900

Like the painting by Sowerby (1876–1914), this belongs to a recognizable "cottage garden school" of minor painters of the late Victorian and Edwardian period. The garden here is slightly larger and more ambitious, as well as less eccentric, than the one depicted by Sowerby. There are traces of Italian influence in the pergola arch and sundial, but the mixed planting, with prominence given to roses, is of a typically English nature.

> *Come into the garden, Maud,*
> *For the black bat, night, has flown,*
> *Come into the garden, Maud,*
> *I am here at the gate alone ...*

ALFRED, LORD TENNYSON (1809–92)

Vincent **VAN GOGH**
Mlle. Gachet in Her Garden (detail)
1890

Mlle. Gachet was the daughter of the homeopathic physician Paul-Ferdinand Gachet, with whom Van Gogh (1853–90) went to stay in 1890, after he discharged himself from the asylum at Saint-Rémy. The doctor lived in the village of Auvers-sur-Oise, just outside Paris. The painting has the fluidity of Van Gogh's very late work—everything seems to move and intermingle...

"*Soft is the music that would charm for ever; The flower of sweetest smell is shy and lowly.*"

WILLIAM WORDSWORTH
(1770–1850)

Annabel **GOSLING**
The Farm in June, Burgundy
1997

A warmly romantic depiction of an old farmhouse and its surroundings in perfect weather in high summer, just at the moment when they seem most seductive to the town dweller.

Sir Hubert Von
HERKOMER
In the Garden (detail)
c. 1890

Herkomer (1849–1914), a naturalized German as his name suggests, was one of the academic "swells" of High Victorian art, like his rivals Leighton (1830–1896) and Alma-Tadema (*see pages 144-5*). He was a specialist in portraits of personages perhaps even grander than himself and this is therefore not a typical example of his work. This is due not only to the subject matter but also the loose handling of paint. The subject is surprisingly close to some of Monet's (1840–1926) pictures of his water garden at Giverny, but Monet would never have included the theatrically posing figure, who may be one of Herkomer's actress friends.

“*Take it from us, it is utterly forbidden to be half-hearted about Gardening. You have got to LOVE your garden, whether you like it or not.*”

W C SELLAR (1898–1951) **AND R J YEATMAN** (1897–1968)

Paul **RANSON**
Foxgloves
1899

Ranson (1864–1909) was one of the founder-members of the Nabis group, who first exhibited together in 1891. The word “Nabi” is Hebrew for “prophet,” and the group, which included Bonnard and Vuillard, saw themselves as the heralds of a new art. The influence of Japanese art was strong in their work. Ranson here combines influences from Japan with the curves of Art Nouveau.

Otto **GEBHARDT**
The Garden
c. 1905

A lithograph from a German children's book, very much in the style of the Swedish artist Carl Larsson (*see page 255*). The design preaches the same cosy domestic virtues that Larsson (1853–1919) espouses, with a mother picking roses with her children, but here the presence in the background of two gardeners doing the heavy work is very striking.

"I would like death to come to me while I am planting cabbages, caring little for death and even less for the imperfection of my garden."

MICHEL EYQUEM DE MONTAIGNE (1533–92)

Dario **REGOYOS Y VALDES**
The Poultry Yard
c. 1900

This painting is in a Spanish version of Neo-Impressionist style. Its charm lies in the meticulous way in which it records a very small domain, evidently seen from a window of the house to which it belongs.

Carlos **FORNS BADA**
Garden VI
1997

The Spanish painter Carlos Forns Bada here constructs a tiny patio garden suitable to the hot, dry climate of many parts of Spain. Subtly stylized, these heat-resistant plants become strange, quasi-surrealist objects.

Kendhal Jan **JUBB**
Window Amaryllis
1999

With this frieze of flowering amaryllis plants in pots, Kendhal Jan Jubb (b. 1957) suggests that the delights of gardening do not have to be completely denied to those who do not own a garden.

Miriam **ESCOFET**
Grande Rose
1999

In this *trompe l'oeil*, the artist suggests that gardening is in some way a sacred occupation, by placing a print of an ecclesiastical rose window within an arch of well-used flowerpots. The title is an elegant pun.

Paul **CÉZANNE**
The Gardener
1905–6

When the aging artist elected to paint human beings, rather than the landscape, his subjects were workmen and servants. His gardener, seated on a kitchen chair in a corner of the painter's domain, seems like an emanation of the soil of Provence.

Charles **ANGRAND**
In the Garden
1885

The painter emphasizes the small size of the plot that the man is cultivating by placing a screen of saplings in front of him and blocking the view to the left with a garden shed. This is a very small patch of ground that can be cultivated in someone's spare time. The fact that this is a leisure activity is emphasized by the man's jaunty black leather cap.

Berthe **MORISOT**
The Lesson in the Garden
1886

Berthe Morisot (1841–95) was living in Jersey in the Channel Islands when she painted this. The little girl in the picture is her daughter Julie Manet, whose recollections of the Impressionist circle have been published comparatively recently.

August **MACKE**
Washing in the Garden in Kandern
1907

The fence in the foreground of the composition signals that this is private ground, while the washing on the line teasingly hints at a kind of voyeuristic intimacy, especially as the two most prominent items seem to be female undergarments.

Camille **PISSARRO**
Woman at Work in a Garden
c. 1890

As usual, Pissarro's (1830–1903) vision of everyday life is more earthy than that of other Impressionists. This woman, dressed in peasant costume, with a scarf tied around her hair, is tilling the heavy soil of a kitchen garden with some effort. Beyond her is a small orchard with a few fruit trees.

Pierre-Auguste
RENOIR
Woman with Parasol in the Garden
1873

The exceedingly overgrown look of this garden was the style favored by Impressionist painters at this time. The flowers in the foreground seem to be an attempt at an English-style herbaceous border, but there is no clear line of demarcation between the border itself and the unmown grassy path that the woman and her companion traverse.

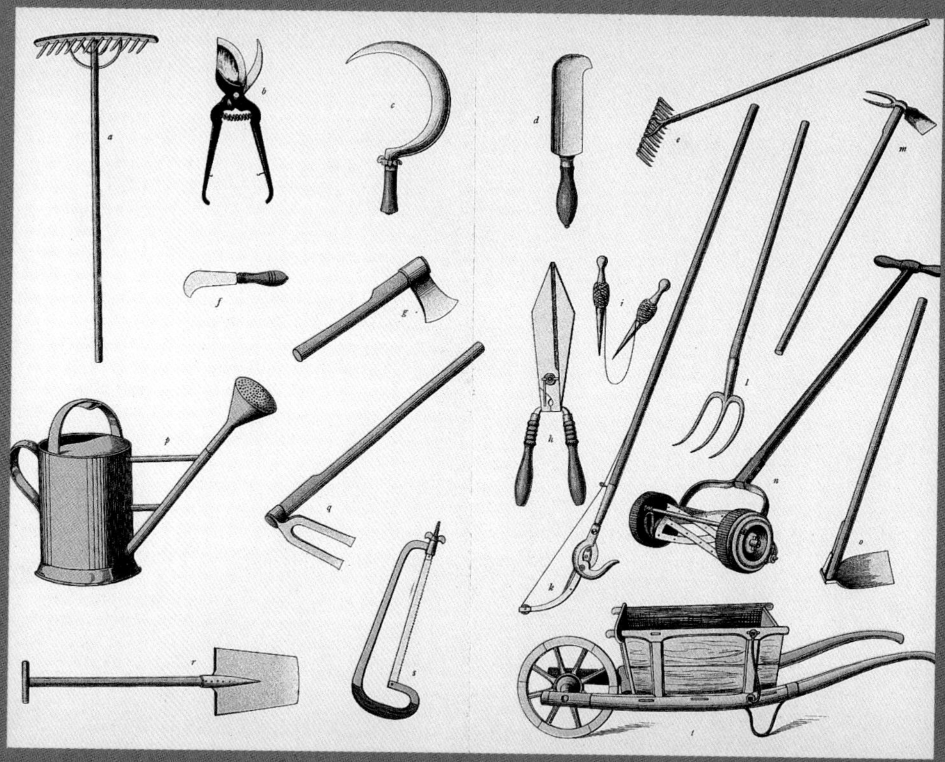

Anthony
HOLDSWORTH
Wheelbarrow
1989

Intense focus on a very ordinary object gives this painting the kind of magic that can also be found in the still lifes that Chardin (1699–1779) painted of mundane kitchen utensils.

Garden Tools, Color Lithograph
1890

An illustration from a late nineteenth-century German book for children, this illustrates common garden utensils of the period. Some of these tools remain much the same today. Others, like the lawnmower and the wheelbarrow, have altered in appearance quite a lot.

"

And here and there were pleasant arbours pight,
And shadie seats, and sundry flowring bankes,
To sit and rest the walkers wearie shanks...

"

EDMUND SPENSER (1552–99)

Édouard **MANET**
Bench, The Garden at Versailles (detail)
1881

Manet (1832–83) rented a villa at Versailles in the year his fatal illness first declared itself. One symptom of this illness was the difficulty he found in walking. This painting records his intense perception of suddenly narrowed surroundings.

CHAPTER TEN

imaginary realms

"Beauteous the garden's umbrage mild,

walk, water, meditated wild, and all the bloomy beds

CHRISTOPHER SMART (1722–71)

Jan **BRUEGEL THE ELDER**
Flora in the Flower Garden
c. 1600

"IMAGINARY GARDENS, with real toads in them" runs the famous line by Marianne Moore (1887–1972). She is, of course, referring to her own poems. Many works of literature can be thought of as realms that the reader is invited to inhabit. An outstanding example is *Le Grand Meaulnes* (1913) by the French writer Alain-Fournier (1886–1914). Based on the writer's own rural childhood, it features a schoolboy hero who runs away and meets a mysterious girl at a party held in a crumbling country house. The rest of the book describes his search for the young woman, and the other-worldly domain that she inhabited.

Mogul artist
The Giant Zamarrad in a Well
(detail)
c. 1570

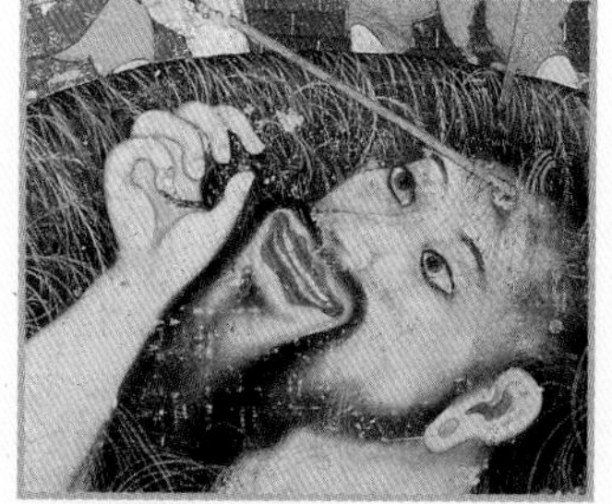

Le Grand Meaulnes is a remote descendant of the early nineteenth-century Gothic novel and its companion, the Oriental romance. *Vathek* (1786) by William Beckford (1766–1844) was originally written in French and tells

of an impious caliph who builds a tower so high that from it he can survey all the kingdoms of the world. Essentially, literary works such as these fascinate readers because the author is re-creating the world in their own image at some level.

Edward Robert
HUGHES
Twilight Fantasies
(detail)
1911

Painters do this even more obviously and this results in the individual stylistic quirks that enable us to distinguish the work of one artist from that of another, even when a picture is unsigned. However, it is more difficult to make a distinction between the imaginary world and the real one when dealing with the visual arts. How much of Claude's (1600–82) idyllic vision of the Campagna is real (*see page 213*), and how much is Arcadian fiction? We know, for example, that in

Sir Peter Paul
RUBENS
The Garden of Love
(detail)
c. 1630–32

Claude's time the area surrounding the city of Rome was depopulated, not merely because of wandering groups of bandits and footpads, but more importantly because of its malarial bogs.

Martha Mayer **ERLEBACHER** *Flora* (detail) 1989

There are artists, however, who seem to make a point of stressing the imaginary or fictional nature of what they depict. No one, for example, would mistake Hieronymous Bosch's (c.1450–1516) *Garden of Earthly Delights* for a literal rendition of what can be seen in nature. The exquisite landscape setting frames a narrative of the first temptation of humankind, and of the Fall. But it also speaks of the dangerous lure of sensuality, and of the different temptations that confront people who live in a pleasure-seeking world.

Hans **ZATSKA** *Amor's Game of Skittles* (detail) Late 19th century

Paradoxically, one of Bosch's most direct successors was

Antoine Watteau (1684–1721). Watteau was the inventor—with a little help from his idol Rubens (1577–1640)—of a new genre, the *fête galante*: an ideal landscape peopled with figures in fashionable contemporary dress. However, often the dress has been adapted from peasant costume and the implication is that his personages are aristocrats playing at the simple life.

Pierre
CHRISTIAN
Dream Fairies
(detail)
1962

Watteau, like Bosch, dwells on the ephemeral nature of earthly pleasure. His *The Embarkation for Cythera*, based very loosely on a contemporary play, shows a group of revelers in a park who are supposedly setting out for the legendary island of love, which is present only as a streak of color on the horizon. The picture is filled with such an atmosphere of melancholy that it has sometimes been interpreted as a departure from Cythera, rather than as the beginning of a journey toward it.

Hunt **SLONEM**
Saint Rose of Lima
(detail)
1989

The first saint of the New World, St. Rose of Lima, is traditionally depicted with a garland of roses in her hair. Legend has it that she hung herself up by her long hair to keep awake for her devotions. Hunt Slonem (b. 1951) goes a step farther than this, by portraying her almost swallowed up by flowers.

Li **SHAN**
Rouge number 1
1989

A contemporary Chinese artist here takes over an idea from the European tradition of fairy painting and depicts flowers with human faces. The borrowing of this subject matter is a typical example of the new eclecticism in contemporary Chinese art.

Amy **SAWYER**
Gentle Spring brings her stuff to market (Detail)
c. 1896

The complete figure shows the artist's debt to her contemporary Sir Edward Burne-Jones (1833–98). The blurring out of the figu face is perhaps intended to symbolize not only the gentleness of the season bu the elusiveness of nature ar natural things, and the way which they escape the gras of human rationality.

"

Then nature said,

'A lovelier flower on earth

was never sown; This child I

to myself will take; She shall

be mine, and I will make

A lady of my own.'

"

WILLIAM WORDSWORTH (1770–1850)

Martha Mayer **ERLEBACHER**
Flora
1989

This is a more typical work by Erlebacher (b. 1937) than the painting shown on page 273. Her *Flora* has real human presence, and the model's expression catches the melancholy and fragility of the flowering season as well as its beauty.

“
There are fairies
at the bottom
of our garden
”

ROSE FYLEMAN (1877–1957)

Pierre **CHRISTIAN**
Dream Fairies
1962

A very late descendant of the fairy paintings of the Victorian epoch, this uses precisely the same elements—tiny winged beings and enlarged flowers.

John George **NAISH**
Midsummer Fairies
c. 1856

Rather earlier than the work by Simmons (1823–76) on page 338, this is another typical Victorian fairy picture. Perhaps its most striking aspect is its disregard for scale. The tiny fairies are among plants—one of them a fuchsia (unromantically named for Leonhard Fuchs, a sixteenth-century German botanist)—that are seen from very close up. Illustrating the fairy realm enabled artists to escape from the demands of Victorian literalism.

> *Waste not your Hour, nor in vain pursuit*
> *Of This and That endeavour and dispute.*
> *Better be jocund with the fruitful Grape*
> *Than sadden after none, or bitter, Fruit.*

EDWARD FITZGERALD (1809–83)

Amelia M. **BOWERLEY or BAUERLE**
At Goblin Harvest
c. 1910

By an artist so obscure that even the exact spelling of her name is uncertain, this carries the "fairy" genre into the Edwardian epoch. The chief influence appears to be Sir John Tenniel's (1820–1914) illustrations to Lewis Carroll's (1832–98) *Alice* books, and, like some of these, it has a slightly sinister quality —are the ripe fruits on offer really as healthy as they seem, given the appearance of those who offer them?

Antoine **WATTEAU**
The Embarkation for Cythera
(detail)
1717

This is perhaps Watteau's (1684–1721) most famous painting—the one that summarizes the nature of the genre he made uniquely his own. Part of the inspiration for Watteau's *fêtes galantes* came from the Italian *commedia dell'arte,* where gestures counted for more than words. However, here the gestures are always ambiguous, as is the mood, which hovers between gaiety and melancholy. Watteau's figures occupy a dream-like realm where the only business is love and love affairs. The outcome is still uncertain, even though the cares of the real world are shut away.

Sir Peter Paul
RUBENS
The Garden of Love
c. 1630–32

Rubens' (1577–1640) famous painting is an allegory of married life. The two figures in the right foreground are the painter himself and his second wife, Helene Fourment, and they are being united by Cupid. The composition is the direct predecessor to Watteau's *fêtes galantes*. It also looks back to illustrations found in the medieval *Roman de la Rose* (*see page 346*).

Jan **BRUEGEL THE ELDER**
and Hendrick **VAN BALEN**
Flora and Nymphs in a Garden
(detail)
Early 17th century

Jan Bruegel the Elder (1568–1625) was the second son of Pieter Bruegel the Elder (1525–69), born only shortly before his father's death. He went on to become a specialist in landscape and flower painting and both specialties are represented here. The figures are the work of another artist, Hendrick van Balen (1575–1632), who was greatly influenced by his exact contemporary, Sir Peter Paul Rubens (1577–1640). The mythological figures van Balen created here are focal points in an idyllic Arcadian realm created by his collaborator. The picture also gives some hints about contemporary gardening techniques—note the plants in pots and urns.

Mogul artist
The Giant Zamarrad in a Well
c. 1570

An illustration from the first great series of Mogul paintings, which was a set of illustrations for the *Hamzanama* or *Romance of Amir Hamza*, painted for the Emperor Akbar (1542–1605). The lush garden setting—depicted with hallucinatory clarity—was to be repeated countless times in later examples of Mogul art.

"*... so full of shapes is fancy,*
That it alone is high fantastical"

WILLIAM SHAKESPEARE (1564–1616)

Salvo **RUSSO**
Horse
1990

This magic horse, bearing a tree on its back, is the kind of image Renaissance allegorists might have devised, though in this contemporary example the actual meaning remains more mysterious than that of most humanist allegories.

John **SIMMONS**
There Sleeps Titania
1872

This is an absolutely typical Victorian "fairy picture," by one of the specialists in the genre. Among its stylistic ancestors is the work of the Pre-Raphaelite Brotherhood, formed over thirty years previously, which had since ceased to be controversial, and that of Henry Fuseli (1741–1825) — Titania reclining on her couch has more than a touch of Fuseli's sensuality. Another source is probably Victorian pantomime.

Elizabeth **SHIPPEN GREEN**
They Call Me Sinbad the Grasshopper
1931

Elizabeth Shippen Green (1871–1954) continued the tradition of children's book illustration that was created, for English-speaking countries, by Kate Greenaway (1846–1901). This picture, from an American children's book, published two years after the Wall Steet crash of 1929, continues to present children's lives as a form of Neo-Regency idyll.

> *Beasts did leap and*
> *birds did sing,*
> *Trees did grow and*
> *plants did spring...*

RICHARD BARNFIELD (1574–1627)

TURNBULL and STOCKDALE
Printed cotton with elves, birds, and dragonflies
1929

Clearly intended for a nursery or children's playroom, this charming commercial fabric design from the end of the 1920s continues the tradition that was originally created for Victorian fairy pictures.

Ubaldo **BARTOLINI**
In the Evening, Especially
1993

Bartolini is a successor of the painters of Arcadian landscapes who flourished in the seventeenth and eighteenth centuries. His images are not meant to be fully realistic, but rather are the expressions of a particular mood.

Angela **VOLPI**
Already from the Treetops
1999

Volpi's Narcissus figure, gazing at himself in the water, seems enchanted by the sounds of nature, which have caused him to abandon the drum that rests beside him.

“*The trees began to whisper, and the wind began to roll, And in the wild March-morning I heard them call my soul.*”

ALFRED, LORD TENNYSON
(1809–92)

Hans **ZATSKA**
Amor's Game of Skittles
Late 19th century

Continental artists do not seem to have practiced the fairy genre as often as their English contemporaries. The alternative, especially toward the end of the century, was a rather camp kind of mythological picture, of which this is an example. The idealized garden setting is delicately painted.

Jon **SWIHART**
Untitled
1991

This is an Arcimboldoesque figure clad in garments adorned with flowers, a hat made of vegetables, and an elaborate staff. The artist's sources for this fantastic apparition seem to include sixteenth- and seventeenth-century drawings for masque costumes.

The Magic Garden, illustration to the Roman de la Rose
Early 16th century

This is one of the illustrations for the great medieval allegory of love by Guillaume de Loris that was one of the most popular French poems of the late Middle Ages. The *Roman de la Rose* contains personifications of Courtesy, Love, Beauty, and Liberality.

Paula **MODERSOHN-BECKER**
The Fairytale Witch
c. 1901

An extremely unusual painting for Modersohn-Becker (1876–1907), this work tries to capture the atmosphere of the fairytales by the Brothers Grimm. It is one of the works in which the artist specifically evokes her German heritage.

Salvo **RUSSO**
Sagittarius
1973

A magical mountain landscape with irrational perspectives, focused on the figure of a nude rider and his horse. Its composition perhaps owes something to Leonardo da Vinci's (1452–1519) *Madonna of the Rocks*.

Edward Robert **HUGHES**
Twilight Fantasies
1911

A belated manifestation of the Pre-Raphaelite spirit, this picture sums up the yearnings of a society that has become weary of all-pervasive industrialism as well as imperialism. The writings of both Rudyard Kipling (1865–1936) and James Barrie (1860–1937) also show this same spirit at different times.

Annabel **LIVERMORE**
My Garden at Dawn
1998–9

Annabel Livermore, allegedly a Texas spinster, never appears at her own exhibition openings, but sends quavery tape-recorded messages instead. This vigorous, quasi-abstract work evokes feelings about the wonder of nature.

Hieronymus **BOSCH**
The Garden of Earthly Delights (Detail)
c. 1504

Bosch (c.1450–1516) is one of the key figures in the transition from the Middle Ages to the Renaissance. His great painting, *The Garden of Earthly Delights,* is a warning against the dreams that afflict people in a pleasure-seeking world, but expresses the warning in images of exquisite sensuality.

index of artists

ALBERTO ABATE
(birthdate unknown)
pages 141 and 148

TOFAT AL-AHRAR
(dates unknown)
pages 180 and 192

SIR LAWRENCE ALMA-TADEMA
(1836–1912)
Originally Dutch, Alma-Tadema took British nationality in 1873. A very successful painter, he specialized in historical series, concentrating on the ancient world, particularly after a trip to Pompeii in 1863. His style is sensuous and the trappings exotic.
pages 141, 144–5, 154–5, 158–9, 169, 193, 215, 216

SILVANO D'AMBROSIO
(b. 1951)
French painter, living and working out of Forli. Widely recognized as the most complete artist of his generation, he attacks landscapes, figures, interiors, and still lifes with the same pictorial strength. The power in his brushstrokes is often enough to carry the entire subject matter of a canvas.
page 237

CHARLES ANGRAND
(1854–1926)
French painter who, in 1884, became a founder member of the Salon des Independants. His early work displayed an Impressionist tendency, but having met Seurat, his style became strictly Neo-Impressionist. He said his rural scenes were "an intellectual vision of harmony."
pages 62–3, 309

GIUSEPPE ARCIMBOLDO
(1527–93)
Milanese painter whose work is instantly recognizable—grotesque

compositions employing vegetation, landscapes, and implements to create human forms. His strangest creations were made for the Hapsburg Emperor Rudolph II in Prague. He was hailed by twentieth-century Surrealists.
page 272

MARIANNE ARNBACK
(birthdate unknown)
page 132

JOHN ATKINSON GRIMSHAW
(1836–93)
English painter best known for his nocturnal townscapes, which are remarkably atmospheric, if rather acidic in color. He worked primarily in his native Leeds and in other northern English towns.
pages 170-1

UBALDO BARTOLINI
(b. 1944)
Italian artist based in Rome and Macerata. Before 1979 his work was defined as conceptual, but by 1980 he had developed a more pictorial style which manifested itself in unreal, enigmatic, and disturbing landscapes.
pages 226 and 342

LUIGI BAZZANI
(1836–1927)
Italian painter born in Bologna, where he also studied. He traveled extensively

through France and Germany before taking up a professorship at the University of Rome.
page 105

SIMON BENING
(1483/4–1561)
Son of the renowned Netherlandish illuminator Sanders Bening, Simon Bening was one of the last great book illuminators, a tradition that died with the arrival of the printing press.
page 64

GINA MARIE BERNARDINI
(b. 1968)
A very versatile American artist from Florida, educated at Rollins College. She is becoming established in galleries throughout the United States.
page 146

CARLO BERTOCCI
(b. 1946)
Italian painter now living and working in Florence. A member of the Pittura Colta (Cultivated Painting) group, he produces timeless visions, characterized by a sensitive and lyrical treatment, that are contemporary representations of myths and heroes of a past era, and also revels in depictions of everyday life where children act as his storytellers.
pages 181, 196–7, 242, 246

ALBERT BIERSTADT
(1830–1902)
German-born American painter, who traveled widely in the United States, when it was still being explored and settled. His grandiose mountain scenes did much to create the myth of the overwhelming splendor of American nature in the minds of his compatriots.
pages 196 and 204

ROBERT BISSELL
(b. 1952)
English-born photographer and artist now living in San Francisco. His canvases are richly colored allegories using flora and fauna. His paintings yield poignant parables reminiscent of the great Victorian illustrators of children's books.
pages 51, 109, 265

DAVID BLAIR
(dates unknown)
page 133

HIERONYMOUS BOSCH
(c.1450–1516)
Netherlandish painter who, despite being an orthodox Catholic, chose bizarre subjects for his paintings; in the seventeenth century the Church declared him a heretic. His grotesque fantasy style is hard to place historically, yet his draughtsmanship and impact on modern art are undeniable.
page 322, 351

FRANÇOIS BOUCHER
(1703–70)
French Rococo painter, engraver, and

designer, whose work best captures the frivolity and elegance of French court life in the mid-eighteenth century. His mastery of decorative and illustrative painting made him extremely successful. The favorite painter of Mme de Pompadour, he did much work both for her and for her royal lover Louis XV.
page 17

BOUCICAUT MASTER
(dates unknown)
pages 60–1

AMELIA M. BOWERLEY or BAUERLE
(dates unknown)
pages 330–1

CHRIS BROUGHTON
(b. 1949)
Active member of a group of artists and writers called the New Arcadians, who publish an annual on gardens and landscapes. Broughton combines teaching, commercial projects, and exhibiting with equal passion, fueled by a lifelong celebration of nature.
pages 84–5

JAN BRUEGEL THE ELDER
(1568–1625)
Flemish painter and draftsman, second son of Pieter Bruegel the Elder, the Netherlands' greatest sixteenth-century painter. Born just a year before his father's death, and therefore little influenced by him. Specialized in still lifes, flowers, and landscapes. His obvious skill with the brush earned him the nickname "Velvet."
pages 143, 152–3, 318, 334–5

PIETER BRUEGEL THE YOUNGER
(1564–1638)
Flemish painter and elder son of Pieter Bruegel. Best known for his copies and variations on his father's peasant themes.
pages 52–3

ELSIE BUNGE
(birthdate unknown)
page 156

SIR EDWARD BURNE-JONES
(1833–98)
English painter, illustrator, and designer. Apprenticed to Rossetti in 1856, who remained his primary influence, although Botticelli was also important. Preferred medieval and mythical subjects and disliked modernists. His work had an influence on the French Symbolists.
pages 213, 224–5

NORTON BUSH
(dates unknown)
page 182-3

JUDY BYFORD
(birthdate unknown)
pages 14 and 30

PAUL CÉZANNE
(1839–1906)
French painter and prime mover of the Post-Impressionist movement, along with Paul Gauguin and Vincent Van Gogh, Cézanne is widely recognized as the father of modern art. Family wealth allowed him to survive the indifference with which his early work was regarded. In his final decade he was adopted as a sage by the avant-garde.
pages 73 and 308

MARC CHAGALL
(1887–1985)
Russian-born painter and designer. Member of an avant-garde circle in Paris which included Apollinaire, Modigliani, and Soutine. A prolific artist and book illustrator, he moved between France, Germany, Russia, and the United States. His work is dominated by the influence of Russian folklore and memories of Jewish life in the Paleov settlement.
pages 142 and 147

ALFRED JEAN CHAGNIOT
(dates unknown)
page 285

WES CHRISTENSEN
(b. 1949)
American artist living and working out of Los Angeles. Christensen creates exceptionally detailed, small-scale, realistic watercolors, as well as contemporary tableaux with strong mythological references and due deference to classical and Old Master images, punctuated with wit and parody.
pages 188, 257, 288–9

PIERRE CHRISTIAN
(dates unknown)
pages 323 and 328

GEORGES CLAIRIN
(1843–1919)
French painter and one of the last successful practitioners of Orientalist painting. Prominent during the 1870s in the decoration of the Paris Opera.
page 198

JAMES COLLINSON
(1825–81)
English watercolorist Collinson studied at the Royal Academy. One of the original Pre-Raphaelite brothers, he was engaged briefly to Christina Rossetti before leaving the movement, and her, to train as a Catholic priest. He later returned to London and art, painting genre subjects in great detail and using bright colors, his early career still having a significant influence upon his

technique. Not regarded as a leading light of the movement; perhaps his greatest talent was being able to fall asleep at any time.
pages 114 and 131

GHISBERT COMBAZ
(1869–1941)
Belgian painter and lithographer who specialized in landscapes.
pages 140 and 157

JEAN-BAPTISTE CAMILLE COROT
(1796–1875)
French painter of landscapes who managed to introduce a new poetic vision into the more classical traditions advocated by the Barbizon school. A great hit at the annual Paris Salon. The popularity of his later work has made him the most forged of all painters.
pages 106–7, 227

LUCAS CRANACH
(1472–1553)
German painter, engraver, and designer of woodcuts, closely associated with the Electoral Court of Saxony and with the Protestant Reformer Martin Luther. He was influenced by Albrecht Dürer; his numerous paintings of female nudes revert to Gothic physical types but nevertheless express a new secularism and sensuality.
page 39

CHARLES CURRAN
(dates unknown)
pages 113, 130–1

WILLIAM DANIELL
(1769–1837)
English painter and engraver. An orphan who was raised by his uncle Thomas, he traveled with him to India for inspiration. Their most beautiful work appeared in the six-volume *Oriental Scenery*, paintings from which appeared at the British Institution and the Royal Academy.
pages 178 and 205

BARBARA DIETZSCH
(1706–83)
German painter, daughter of Johann Israel, most renowned for her paintings of flowers and animals. The use of a black background is typical of her work.
page 137

ARTHUR DIXON
(dates unknown)
pages 14, 36–7

MARTHA MAYER ERLEBACHER
(b. 1937)
One of North America's most respected figurative painters, Erlebacher lives and works in Pennsylvania, teaches in New York, and lectures throughout the United States. Her still lifes are much praised, combining acute observation with inspired composition.
pages 273, 322, 327

MIRIAM ESCOFET
(b. 1967)
Originally from Barcelona, Escofet is now resident in England.
Her watercolors and ceramics, characterized by a mesmeric attention to detail, have been exhibited widely throughout Europe and in America.
page 307

STEFANIA FABRIZI
(birthdate unknown)
Italian artist, born, educated, and now based in Rome. One of Alberto Ziveri's last pupils. Her favorite subject is Man and her influences include Piero della Francesca, Ingres, and the sculptor Canova. Her style evokes an intense spiritual longing.
page 168

JOSE FILLOL
(dates unknown)
pages 243 and 258

GEORG FLEGEL
(1566–1638)
German painter who started work under Lucas van Valeckenborch I (1540–97). His early watercolors of animals, flowers, and fruit are in the tradition of Dürer, and develop into the "high horizon" compositions featuring numerous scattered objects which are typical of the first generation of Dutch still-life painters, from whom his work is inseparable. Human figures are rare in his work.
pages 266–7

CARLOS FORNS BADA
(birthdate unknown)
Spanish painter from Madrid, a leading exponent of Spanish and indeed

European figurative painting. The warm tones of his palette blend effortlessly the spiritual and metaphysical aspects of his subjects, while, marked by a strong, plastic quality, and bathed in light, his pictures evoke a timeless atmosphere.
pages 195, 263, 305

ELEANOR FORTESCUE-BRICKDALE
(1871–1945)
English painter regarded for her book illustrations, particularly for Edwardian gift books. Commissioned to illustrate Tennyson's poems and *Idylls of the King* and Browning's *Pippa Passes*. Exhibited regularly at the Royal Academy.
pages 142, 172–3

LESLEY FOTHERBY
(b. 1947)
English watercolorist and one-time teacher, now living in Yorkshire. She exhibits regularly at the Royal Horticultural Society.
pages 122–3

ROBERT FURBER
(dates unknown)
page 264

IAN GARDNER
(b. 1944)
A British artist with a long and distinguished career as a teacher on both sides of the Atlantic, Gardner is also widely exhibited and collected. His concern for gardens and landscapes is the primary motivation of his art.
pages 79, 86, 282, 290–1

PAUL GAUGUIN
(1848–1903)
French Post-Impressionist painter, sculptor, and print-maker, and companion of Vincent Van Gogh in Arles. He is most renowned for the primitive vigor of his work post-1891, when he left France for Tahiti. His illustrated book *Noa Noa* describes his time there, romantically envisioning his artistic escape from civilized conventions.
pages 241, 248, 250–1, 256–7

OTTO GEBHARDT
(dates unknown)
page 303

ANNABEL GOSLING
(b. 1942)
An English artist whose travels through Europe and India have influenced her palette and her use of light to evoke atmosphere. In fact, her obsession with light and the way it saturates her work could be considered to be her trademark.
pages 280, 284, 300

BENOZZO GOZZOLI
(c. 1421–97)
A Florentine painter who trained as a goldsmith and worked with Ghiberti on the doors of the Baptistry in Florence. He became assistant to Fra Angelico in Rome and Orvieto. His reputation rests on the decoration of the Chapel of the Palazzo Medici in Florence.
page 166

EUGENE SAMUEL GRASSET
(1841–1917)
French illustrator, decorative artist, and printmaker in Switzerland. A leading figure in Art-Nouveau poster design, he also showed a keen interest in the dramatic representation of women.
pages 213, 218–9

KATE GREENAWAY
(1846–1901)
English artist and writer famous for her illustrations for children's books. Legend has it that the clothes in which she portrayed her characters inspired a contemporary fashion.
pages 286–7

WILLIAM HAVELL
(1782–1857)
Self-taught British landscape painter, founder member of the Society of Painters in Watercolor. In 1816 he accepted the position of official artist to the embassy in China under William Pitt, but he also traveled in South America and India.
pages 178, 184–5

MARTIN JOHNSON HEADE

(1819–1904)

American painter, originally of portraits but later of meticulous and restrained landscapes full of atmosphere. Inspired by trips to Central and South America, he produced a series of still lifes, orchids, and hummingbirds, which fused his love of landscapes and still life.

pages 116–7

DOROTHY HENRIQUES WELLS

(birthdate unknown)

Senior Jamaican artist, celebrated as one of the finest watercolorists in the Americas. She is greatly influenced by the vibrant colors and vegetation of the Caribbean. The freshness of her work is both expressive, lyrical, delicate, and sensitive to abstract values.

pages 129 and 203

SIR HUBERT VON HERKOMER

(1849–1914)

English painter born in Bavaria. He was a versatile artist, best known for his portraits and scenes of social concern.

page 301

F. SCOTT HESS

(b. 1955)

Having studied at the Academy of Fine Art in Vienna, Austria, Hess was strongly influenced by the German Expressionists. Upon returning to his native Los Angeles, his trademark work began to take on strong narrative sense, as he celebrates everyday life with a darkly theatrical mood.

pages 106 and 119

ANDO HIROSHIGE

(1797–1858)

Japanese painter and print-maker, and eldest son of a Samurai. Hiroshige xperimented with naturalistic and

Western-influenced styles of the Nagasaki and Shijo schools, but ultimately followed in the Ukiyo-e genre under Toyoiro. His views of Mount Fuji and Edo remain intimate examples of his finest work.

page 202

KATUSHIKA HOKUSAI

(1760–1849)

Japanese master artist and print-maker of the Ukiyo-e school, Hokusai was also one of the major erotic picture makers of the Edo period. His sequential collections of landscapes are not exact depictions of nature but images from the artist's inner world. He is believed to be the first Japanese artist to have used Prussian blue.

page 124

ANTHONY HOLDSWORTH

(b. 1945)

American artist born in England, Holdsworth now exhibits and teaches extensively in Central and South America. Working *en plein air* on urban themes, he is well regarded as a colorist, and produces very atmospheric work.

pages 276 and 315

EDWARD ROBERT HUGHES

(1851–1914)

English painter based in London, who studied at the Royal Academy with Holman Hunt. His romantic genre paintings, often with subjects drawn from the work of the Italian poet Boccaccio, are his most respected works.

pages 321, 348–9

JAN VAN HUYSUM

(1682–1749)

Dutch painter who, along with Rachel Ruysch, was the most distinguished flower painter of his day, with a pan-European reputation. His light palette and the openness of his compositions set the standard for his peers.

page 152

ICHIMYOSAI
(dates unknown)
pages 162-3

SIR EDWARD AUGUSTUS INGLEFIELD
(1820–94)
English amateur painter also famous for inventing the Inglefield anchor. He was chairman of the Arts section of the Chelsea Naval Exhibition of 1891, and exhibited at the Royal Academy.
pages 199-201

KENDHAL JAN JUBB
(b. 1957)
Montana artist celebrating the nature of her native state, as well as the exotica of Hawaii. Her renderings of opulent flowers and wild animals are often juxtaposed with domestic scenes.
pages 206 and 306

FERDINAND VON KNAB
(dates unknown)
pages 20–1

JACQUES DE LAJOUE
(dates unknown)
page 233

CARL LARSSON
(1853–1919)
Swedish painter and graphic artist who produced predominantly large-scale murals, although his greatest impact and legacy stem from his intimate watercolor treatments of perfect everyday life at his home in Dalecarlia. He is the progenitor of today's "Swedish style" in interior decoration.
page 255

MICHAEL LEONARD
(b. 1933)
Having studied at St. Martin's School of Art, London, Leonard worked initially as an illustrator, and his first paintings were not exhibited until 1972. Better known for his nudes, he produces an occasional still life. Since the mid-1980s he has worked in oils, his technique broadening in effect as his compositions have grown more monumental, the frame's bounding edge playing a crucial role in the composition.
pages 240, 262, 277

JOHN F. LEWIS
(1805–76)
English painter famous for his

exquisitely detailed Oriental scenes He traveled widely in the Middle East to collect material. Son of the landscape painter and engraver Frederick Christian Lewis (1779–1856).
pages 6, 179, 199

LOYSET LIEDET
(c.1420–79)
Late fifteenth-century South Netherlandish illuminator whose increasingly crude work represents the decline of a once-great school of artists while still retaining a certain charm.
page 27

DAVID LIGARE
(b. 1945)
American painter living and working from a studio amid the Gabilan Mountains in California. Involved with nature, his work celebrates his "back yard" and the Californian landscape in general, while insisting on symmetry and mathematical proportion.
pages 99, 210–11, 212

ANNABEL LIVERMORE
(birthdate unknown)
An elderly Texan painter, never seen at her own exhibition openings, though she sometimes sends quavery tape-recorded greetings. She "inhabits the same body" as the well-known Texas avant-garde sculptor, Jim McGee, who lives in El Paso.
pages 350–1

RICHARD LOPEZ
(b. 1943)
American artist of Hispanic origin working and teaching in California. His work reflects an ethnic sensibility, capturing migrant worker life within their Pacific landscape in an earthy palette evoking the bounty of nature.
page 67

JANE LOUDON
(dates unknown)
page 126

AUGUST MACKE
(1887–1914)
German Expressionist painter who managed to create his own personal, somewhat French, style through the synthesis of Impressionism, Fauvism, and Orphism. He formed Der Blaue Reiter with Wassily Kandinsky and Franz Marc, but remained a reluctant abstractionist.
pages 44, 46–7, 78, 83, 311

ÉDOUARD MANET
(1832–83)
Great French painter and graphic artist who, although cast as a classic rebel, was very much a product of his upper-middle-class background. Admired by the Impressionists Monet, Renoir, Bazille, Sisley, and latterly Cézanne, he remained aloof, preferring to go to the races with Degas, who was closer to his own social background. Manet is viewed as one of the founders of modern art.
pages 148–9, 316–7

ALEXANDER MANN
(1853–1908)
Scottish painter who studied in Paris and was influenced by Impressionism before settling in England. He is best known for his views of the Downs.
pages 42 and 55

TITO MARCI
(b. 1966)
Italian artist singled out by the respected critic Italo Mussa, who defined the emerging Pittura Colta movement in contemporary Italian art. In the early 1990s his work centered on the self-portrait as self-analysis. His recent works show a refreshing shift to Giottoesque representation of landscape.
pages 220–2

THOMAS FALCON MARSHALL
(1818–78)
English painter of portraits, landscapes, historical, and conversation pieces. He worked in Manchester and Liverpool and in 1846 was elected a member of the Liverpool Academy. He first exhibited at the Royal Academy in 1839.
page 171

ROBERTO MARQUEZ
(b. 1959)
Mexican figurative artist now resident in New Jersey. His deeply lyrical subjects are wide open to interpretation, drawing on poetic, operatic, and mythical sources. Although often aligned with the early twentieth-century Symbolists, his work is deeply influenced by his own cultural heritage.
page 108

ALFREDO RAMOS MARTINEZ
(1872–1946)
Mexican artist who studied in Paris before turning to teaching; established the Escuelas de Pintura al Aire Libre. Moved from a romantic European style toward Mexican realism, though he portrays his people in idealized settings bearing produce from the their labors.
pages 8 and 249

HENRI MATISSE
(1869–1954)
French painter, sculptor, graphic artist, and designer, the leading figure in the Fauve group. Following World War 1 his stature was equaled only by

that of Picasso. A visionary working with color and line; perhaps his greatest work remains the Chapel of the Rosary in Venice which displays every aspect of his art.
page 253

JACQUELYN MCBAIN
(b. 1954)
American artist preoccupied by the microcosms created by flora. With her exquisitely detailed predatory insects amid flowers, she hints, somewhat uncomfortably, at the battles between nature and technology, and between man and woman.
page 247

ARTHUR MELVILLE
(1855–1904)
Scottish Impressionist. His early works of peasants were painted in a subdued palette, but he developed a coloristic watercolor style, which remained his medium of choice.
pages 69 and 102

PAULA MODERSOHN-BECKER
(1876–1907)
German painter and graphic designer. A member of the Worpswede School, she became dissatisfied with the sentimentalized manner of the group, and developed a more economical style making her the precursor of German Expressionism. She is best remembered for her symbolic use of color and the primitive energy within her work.
pages 244, 346–7

CLAUDE MONET
(1840–1926)
Archetypal French Impressionist painter, devoted to painting outdoors. His celebrated series of "Grainstacks," painted at different times of the day in different lights, was profoundly influential. Perhaps best remembered for his "Water Lilies" series, inspired by his celebrated water-garden at Giverny.
pages 40–1

RENAUD DE MONTAUBAN
(dates unknown)
pages 26-7

BERTHE MORISOT
(1841–95)
French Impressionist painter. Product

of a very cultured background, she was a student of Jean-Baptiste Camille Corot but ultimately more influenced by Manet, whose brother she married. Most loved for her intimate domestic scenes often featuring members of her family.
pages 310–11

WILLIAM MORRIS
(1834–96)
He married Jane Burden, who became the Pre-Raphaelite painter Dante Gabriel Rossetti's archetypal femme fatale muse. He founded the manufacturing and decorating firm Morris, Marshall, Faulkner & Co in 1861, some of whose wallpaper designs are still commercially manufactured worldwide today.
pages 274–5

MAUD NAFTEL
(1856–90)
Victorian painter based in London, predominantly producing landscapes and floral subjects. She exhibited between 1875 and 1896, showing some work at the Royal Academy.
pages 292–4

JOHN NAISH
(dates unknown)
pages 328–9

JOHN NAVA
(b. 1947)
American painter, best known for his representational work, producing nudes and floral still lifes that have become standard for the genre. His work is very collectable. He is currently working on *The Communion of Saints* for the long-awaited Cathedral of Our Lady of the Angels in Los Angeles.
pages 136 and 268

a happy balance between observation and lyricism.
pages 304–5

PIERRE-AUGUSTE RENOIR
(1841–1919)
Renoir was a French Impressionist painter and a close friend of Monet. Renoir's predilection for frivolous themes was influenced by the Rococo masters he studied in Paris. He is arguably the most popular of all the Impressionist painters and his treatment of pretty children, beautiful scenes, flowers, and attractive women have a timeless, universal appeal.
pages 43, 64–5, 115, 121, 278–9, 283, 312–3

LITHIAN RICCI
(birthdate unknown)
Roman artist now resident in Milan. Having acquired a degree in architecture, Ricci attended Heatherly School of Fine Arts in London. She produces vivid fairytale scenes, often breaking free from the confines of the canvas and extending over the frame to create seductive, disturbing fantasies.
pages 96–7, 164

JACQUES RIGAUD
(1681–1754)
French painter producing, predominantly, views of French palaces.
pages 100–1

ERASMUS RITTER VON ENGERT
(1798–1871)
Born in Vienna, von Engert worked at the Academie, before traveling to Italy. When he returned to Austria, he concentrated on picture restoration, becoming conservator at the Galerie du Belvedere, although he also produced good copies of the Old Masters, some portraits, and some history paintings.
page 295

THOMAS ROBINS
(dates unknown)
pages 82–3

ALFRED ROLL
(dates unknown)
pages 10–11

FRANK ROMERO
(dates unknown)
page 187

THOMAS MATTHEWS ROOKE
(1842–1942)
Second generation Pre-Raphaelite and follower of Burne-Jones, whom he was happy to assist until the artist's death. Encouraged by Ruskin, he went to France and Italy, countries that eventually brought out the best in him.
pages 234-5

DANTE GABRIEL ROSSETTI
(1828–82)
English painter and poet, from an extraordinarily literary family. In 1848 he formed the Pre-Raphaelite brotherhood with Hunt and Millais. The death of his wife Elizabeth Siddal affected him profoundly, and the *femmes fatales* that dominated his work often reflected her haunting beauty. Others reflect the beauty of his mistress, Jane Morris, wife of the poet and designer William Morris, while others still are images of another mistress, the robust and voluptuous Fanny Cornforth.
page 155

HENRI ROUSSEAU

(1844–1910)

This French artist was an exponent of the Naïve style of painting. Wholly self-taught, he took up painting late in life, and was briefly fêted by the avant-garde; although historically categorized as the archetypal untutored artist, his work has also been much ridiculed by critics. He favored exotic subject matter, and his palette was extraordinarily bright, which lent an almost theatrical and decorative sense to the deadpan, two-dimensional quality of the creatures he portrayed. While Paul Gauguin traveled to the South Seas, Rousseau's experience of the exotic was limited to his visits to the hothouses of Paris. His nickname "le Douanier" refers only to his time as a customs officer.

pages 206-7, 242, 271

ERNEST ARTHUR ROWE

(1862–1922)

A painter of landscapes and gardens, many of them in Italy. His work has often been criticized for being over-detailed.

pages 80, 98, 104–5

SIR PETER PAUL RUBENS

(1577–1640)

Flemish painter, designer, and diplomat, the undisputed king of Baroque art in northern Europe. The breadth of his subject matter made him hugely influential for subsequent generations of artists. Constable, though, was perhaps correct to single out his landscapes for exceptional praise.

pages 321 and 333

SALVO RUSSO

(b. 1954)

Italian painter who lives and works in Catania, where he teaches at the Academia di Belle Arti. He fuses his conscious influences—drawn from International Gothic, metaphysics, and Surrealism—to create strikingly bold compositions.

pages 28–9, 90–1, 228, 337, 348

JOHN SINGER SARGENT

(1856–1925)

American painter born to wealthy cosmopolitan parents, famous for his portraits of high society. The writer William Starkweather correctly described him as "an American born in

Italy, educated in France, who looks like a German, speaks like an Englishman, and paints like a Spaniard."

pages 76–7, 254

GIOVANNI BATTISTA SALVI (SASSOFERATO)

(1609–85)

Italian painter, known by the name of the town of his birth. Specialized in religious works which he executed in a sweet, almost Peruginoesque style; his work was consciously un-Baroque. Very little is known about his private life and most of his work was undated.

page 173

LILY SALVO

(birthdate unknown)

pages 7 and 160

AMY SAWYER

(dates unknown)

page 326

PAUL SERUSIER

(1844–1927)

French painter and art theorist. Having met Gauguin, he adopted a Symbolist stance, before founding the Nabis with Bonnard and Vuillard. He wrote the influential volume *ABC de la Peinture* in 1921, which dealt with systems of proportion and color; indeed, he was perhaps more highly regarded for his theories than his art.

pages 238–9

LI SHAN

(birthdate unknown)

Modern Chinese painter resident in Shanghai, whose work forms part of the Political Pop movement, though with

more fantasy and less political comment than that of some of his colleagues.
page 325

ELIZABETH SHIPPEN GREEN
(1871-1954)
page 339

HENRYK SIEMIRADZKI
(1843–1902)
Polish painter best known for his academic classicism, especially scenes from classical antiquity and episodes from the lives of early Christians, who were executed on a monumental scale. His compositions are rich in drama and pathos, with much decorative detail.
pages 214 and 217

JOHN SIMMONS
(1823-76)
page 338

HUNT SLONEM
(b. 1951)
American painter established in New York City. His spacious apartment houses an aviary affording him instant access to inspiration for his tropical bird canvases. All his work is richly exotic in content and color.
pages 7, 112, 117, 176-7, 324

LARRY SMART
(birthdate unknown)
An English artist brought up in the Middle East and then educated at Croydon Art School. Important commissions include a series of murals for ex-Beatle George Harrison. He admits to being greatly influenced by his childhood memories of the Middle East, and by time spent recently in Marrakesh.
page 87

NANCY SMITH
(dates unknown)
page 53

JOHN GEORGE SOWERBY
(1876–1914)
English landscape painter who exhibited regularly at the Royal Academy.
pages 296–7

STEFANO DI STASIO
(b. 1948)
Italian painter now living and working in Rome. His unconventional training has freed his work somewhat, although his early years saw him preoccupied by High Renaissance painting traditions. He is now generally regarded as one of the Anacronisti, who look to aspects of the Italian past for artistic inspiration.
pages 92, 161, 260

EDWARD STOTT
(1859–1918)
pages 66–7

GEORGE STUBBS
(1724–1806)
English engraver and animal painter regarded as the greatest painter of horses. Largely self-taught, it was his book *The Anatomy of the Horse*, published in 1766, that really launched his career. Primarily classified as a superior sporting artist during his lifetime, but history has elevated his talent to the front row alongside contemporaries Reynolds and Gainsborough.
pages 54–5

JON SWIHART
(b. 1954)
This contemporary Californian artist is known for atmospheric allegorical paintings, in which he combines a

strong narrative with an acute eye for detail, while paying homage to the Old Masters.
page 345

ALBERT TOLLER
(dates unknown)
page 103

KITAGAWA UTAMARO
(dates unknown)
page 125

VINCENT VAN GOGH
(1853–90)
Prodigious Dutch painter and the paradigm of the romantic ideal of artistic obsession, madness, and genius. He sold only one painting during his lifetime. The speed at which he worked for a long time blinded people to the awesome emotional content with which his paintings were imbued.
pages 75, 79, 89, 110–1, 281, 298–9

JAN VAN KESSEL THE ELDER
(1626–79)
Flemish still life and flower painter. Continued the traditions of his grandfather, Jan "Velvet" Bruegel. Best known for his works depicting garlands and bouquets of flowers, and for his jewel-like insects and shells, often painted on copper.
page 223

THEO VAN RYSSELBERGHE
(1862–1926)
Belgian painter, designer, and sculptor. One-time pupil of Jean-François Portaels, director of the Academie Royaux des Beaux-Arts in Brussels, van Rysselberghe was well traveled; he drew stylistically from his meetings with Whistler and Seurat in 1886, his later work displaying Neo-Impressionist characteristics.
pages 281 and 294

LUCAS VAN VALKENBORCH
(c.1530–97)
Member of a famous family of Netherlandish landscape and genre painters. He traveled extensively with his brother through Italy, working in the Bruegel tradition.
pages 260–1

JOSÉ MARIA VELASCO
(1840–1912)
The most respected Mexican landscape painter of the nineteenth century. His large output featured his own country predominantly, though his horizons broadened in later life.
page 208

CLAUDE-JOSEPH VERNET
(1714–89)
One of three distinguished French painters from the same family. A leading landscape artist who, along with Hubert Robert, became a prominent exponent of an idealized style which was overly sentimental but hugely popular at the time. Also recognized for his seashores. Louis XV commissioned him to paint a series of famous French ports.
page 236

STEFANO DA VERONA
(c.1375–1451)
Italian painter with a hazy biography, believed to have worked in Lombardy. He is a representative of the International Gothic style which flourished at the beginning of the fifteenth century. His early works appear flat and decorative, but in later life he adopted a more naturalistic approach, introducing a greater sense of narrative.
pages 15 and 23

JOSEPH-MARIE VIEN
(1716–1809)
French painter and self-appointed pioneer of the Neoclassical style. Winner of the much-acclaimed Prix de Rome. His classicism was, however, viewed with suspicion as he tended to

sentimentalize his subject matter and then overload it with pseudo-antique trappings. Napoleon made him a senator after the Revolution.
pages 9 and 165

ANGELA VOLPI
(birthdate unknown)
pages 287 and 343

CHU HING WAH
(birthdate unknown)
Chinese watercolourist, resident in Hong Kong, who endeavors to combine a modernist vision, influenced by Western artists like Matisse, with age-old Chinese traditions going back to the Sung Dynasty.
page 127

HENRY WALLIS
(1830–1916)
English artist, writer, and collector. He specialized in portraits of literary figures and scenes from the lives of past artists and his historical genre paintings suggest that he was greatly influenced by, although never a member of, the Pre-Raphaelite brotherhood.
page 118

ERNEST WALBOURN
(dates unknown)
Lesser-known English artist who exhibited works at the Royal Academy.
page 297

JOHN WILLIAM WATERHOUSE
(1849–1917)
English painter best remembered for his distinctive, romantic style. Influenced by the Pre-Raphaelites, but technically very different from them, for he preferred a richer, more sensuous brushstroke. His work includes some classic Victorian literary anthology pieces such as *The Lady of Shalott* and *Hylas and the Nymphs*.
pages 43 and 47

ANTOINE WATTEAU
(1684–1721)
A central figure in the history of Rococo art, inventor of the *fête galante*, and the leading painter of his generation in France. The dreamy, pastoral settings of many of his works, coupled with a lazy romanticism, were to become a stylistic trademark, while his use of pale, translucent color was inspirational.
pages 38 and 332

MICHAEL WENTZEL
(dates unknown)
pages 241 and 245

DAVID WILLETTS
(b. 1939)
British painter whose work centers around the endless cycles and layers of time and space within the natural world. He draws his subjects from three categories—the earth, creatures, and plants—and depicts them in a continuous repetitive narrative of change, decay, and renewal.
page 120

HANS ZATSKA
(1859–1945)
page 345

picture credits

AKG LONDON 25, 103, 186, 217, 244, 252, 258, 259, 311, 312, 318-319, 344, 347 / Alte Nationalarchiv f. Kunst & Geschichte, Berlin 20, 286, 303, 314 / Alte Nationalgalerie, Berlin 295 / Kunstmuseum, Basel 207 / Cason del Buen Retiro 304 / Musee du Petit Palais, Geneva 62 / India House Office Library 274 / Kunsthandel, Berlin 83 / Eric Lessing 38, 165, 167, 272 / Museum der Bildenden Kunste, Leipzig 245 / Jean Louis Nou 32 / Museum am Ostwall, Dortmund 46 / Musee du Petit Palais, Paris 73 / Musee Nat. de l'Hotel de Cluny, Paris 24 / Musee des Beaux-Arts, Orleans 248 / Prado, Madrid, Spain 351 / Private Collection, Switzerland 65 / Sammlung Thyssen-Bornemisza 313 / Staatliches Kunstmuseum, Bukarest 52 / Tate Gallery, London 271 / Vatican Museum, Rome 269 / Biblioteca di San Marco, Venice 64;

ALBERMARLE GALLERY, LONDON / Miriam Escofet 307 / Annabel Gosling 284, 300;

MARIANNE ARNBACK 132;

BRIDGEMAN ART LIBRARY, London/New York 205 / Ashmolean Museum, Oxford, UK 131, 158-159, 234-235 / Museo D'Arte Moderno di ca Pesaro, Venice, Italy 253 / Musee des Beaux-Arts, Rouen, France 230-231, 233, 309 / Chris Beetles Ltd, London, UK 94-95, 122-123 / Bibliotheque de L'Arsenal, Paris, France 26 / Bibliotheque Nationale, Paris, France 60-61, 128 / Bibliotheque Royale de Belgique, Brussels 19 / Birmingham Museums & Art Gallery , UK 118 / Bonham's, London, UK 137, 301 / City of Bristol Museum & Art Gallery, Avon, UK 193, 224-225 / British Library, London, UK 50, 74, 202 / British Museum, London, UK 174-175 / Burhrle Collection, Zurich, Switzerland 308 / Musee Carnavalet, Paris, France 150 / Cheltenham Art Gallery & Museums, Glos, UK 82 / Chester Beatty Library and Gallery of Oriental Art, Dublin 190-191 / Christie's, London, UK 36-37, 47, 121, 196, 250-251, 260-261, 278-279, 294 / City Museum & Art Gallery, London, UK 58 / Musee Conde, Chantilly, France 35 / Russell-Cotes Art Gallery & Museum, Bournemouth, UK 155, 172, 326 / David David Gallery, Philadelphia, USA 204 / Musee D'Orsay, France 40, 149, 298-299 / Galerie L'Ergastere, Paris, France 302 / Earl of Pembroke Collection , Wilton House, UK 173 / Fine Art Society, London, UK 55 / Fitzwilliam Museum, Cambridge University, UK 125 / J Paul Getty Museum, Malibu, CA, USA 110-111 / Giraudon, Musee des Beaux-Arts, Besancon, France 17 / Harris Museum & Art Gallery, Preston, Lancashire, UK 170, 199 / Hermitage St Petersburg 346 / Imperial War Museum, London, UK 254 / Kunsthistorisches Museum, Vienna 39 / Lindley Library, RHS, London, UK 162 / Louvre, Paris, France 107, 227, 332 / Galerie Daniel Malingue, Paris, France 70-71, 147 / The Maas Gallery, London, UK 349 / Collection of Andrew McIntosh Patrick, UK 69 / Roy Miles Esq 54 / Mogao Caves, Dunhuang, Gansu Province, NW China 59 / Nardoni Gallery, Prague 208 / National Gallery, London 138-139 / National Library of Australia, Canberra 194 / Noortman. London, UK 152 / John Noot Galleries, Broadway, Worcs, UK 219, 285 / Palazzo Medici-Riccardi, Florence 166 / Phillips, The Fine Art Auctioneers, London, UK 93, 134-135, 297 / Prado, Madrid, Spain 333 / Private Collection 31, 34, 48-49, 56-57, 87, 100-101, 104, 116, 130, 145, 151, 154, 169, 182-183, 184-185, 192, 216, 232, 238-239, 255, 266-267, 275,

310-311, 330-331, 334-335, 338, 339 / Pushkin Museum, Moscow, Russia 75, 237, 256 / Oskar Reinhart Collection, Winterthur, Switzerland 89 / Royal Geographical Society, London 200-201 / Sheffield Galleries & Museums Collections, UK 66 / Sotheby's London 153 / Stadelsches Kunstinstitut, Frankfurt-Am-Main, Germany 22 / Stapleton Collection 53 / Valley of the Nobles, Thebes, Egypt 72 / Johnny Van Haeften Gallery, London. UK 223 / Victoria & Albert Museum, London, UK 16, 68, 76-77, 88, 124, 126, 163, 264, 336, 340-341 / Waterhouse & Dodd, London, UK 105 / Peter Willi, Hotel de Ville, Paris, France / Whitford & Hughes, London, UK 157, 198 / Christopher Wood Gallery, London, UK 98, 102, 171, 292-293, 296, 329;

CHRIS BROUGHTON 84-85;

IAN GARDNER 86, 290, 291;

HANART TZ GALLERY / Chu Hing Wah 127 / Li Shan 325;

MICHAEL LEONARD 262, 276;

DAVID LIGARE 99, 210-211;

ANNABEL LIVERMORE 350;

LIZARDI/HARP GALLERY, Los Angeles / Robert Bissell 51, 109, 265 / Wes Christensen 188, 257, 288-289 / Martha Erlebacher 273, 327 / Scott Hess 106, 119 / Anthony Holdsworth 276, 315 / Kendhal Jan Jubb 206, 306 / Richard Lopez 67 / Jacquelyn McBain 247 / John Nava 136, 268 / Robin Palanker 222 / Hank Pitcher 33, 183, 209 / Frank Romero 187 / Hunt Slonem 2, 117, 176-177, 324 / John Swihart 345;

IL POLITICO / Silvano d'Ambrosio 237 / Ubaldo Bartolini 226, 342 / Carlo Bertocci 197, 246 / Carlos Forns Bada 195, 263, 305 / Tito Marci 220-221 / Salvatore Pulvirenti 189, 229 / Lithian Ricci 96, 97, 164 / Salvo Russo 28, 90-91, 228, 337, 348 / Lily Salvo 160 / Stefano Di Stasio 92, 161, 260 / Angela Volpi 287, 343;

DAVID SQUIRES 133;

SUPERSTOCK 18, 146, 328 / Musee des Artes Decoratifs, Paris, France 218 / Museo Castelvecchio, Verona, Italy, Canail Photobank, Milan 23 / Christie's Images 249, 316-317 / The Grand Design, Leeds 30 / Kactus Foto, Santiago, Chile 156;

VERJO / Alberto Abate 148 / Stefania Fabrizi 168;

DOROTHY HENRIQUES WELLS 129, 203;

DAVID WILLETS 120;

RIVA YARES GALLERY / Roberto Marquez 108;

DACS 2000, 2, 40, 117, 147, 176-177, 253, 324.

ACKNOWLEDGEMENTS

The author would like to thank Massimo Caggiano and Arnaldo Romani Brizzi of Il Politico.

TEXT ACKNOWLEDGEMENTS

For the following quotations: "But Peter, who was very naughty..." extract from "The Tale of Peter Rabbit" by Beatrix Potter. Copyright © Frederick Warne & Co., 1902, 1987. Reproduced with kind permission of Frederick Warne & Co; "There are fairies..." by Rose Fyleman. Reproduced with kind permission of The Society of Authors; "I, with as easy hunger take..." by Laurie Lee. Reprinted by permission of the Peters Fraser & Dunlop Group; "Take it from us..." extract from "Garden Rubbish" by W C Sellar and R J Yeatman. Reproduced with kind permission of E J Quick and B Yeatman.